LEARN *to* ORGANIZE

Cover Design and Interior Illustrations: Julie Lindstrom
Copy Editors: Ann Kohler & Kristina Fortune Anderson

LEARN *to* ORGANIZE

A PROFESSIONAL ORGANIZER'S TELL-ALL GUIDE TO HOME ORGANIZING

Sara Pedersen

table of contents

INTRODUCTION

ORGANIZING SMALL, SIMPLE SPACES

ORGANIZING COMPLEX PROJECTS

ORGANIZING PAPERWORK & PHOTOS

CLUTTER & MAINTENANCE TIPS

APPENDIX

CONCLUSION

introduction

welcome message

Thank you for purchasing this book! It is a long-awaited companion to my first book, *Born to Organize: Everything You Need to Know About a Career as a Professional Organizer*. If you haven't yet read it, I highly encourage you to check it out if you are a new or prospective professional organizer. It covers all the important business start-up information needed to get a successful organizing business up and running.

This new book, *Learn to Organize*, is a "how-to" of the actual hands-on organizing process. No doubt, you've read dozens of books that share tips on how to organize this space or that. But *Learn to Organize* is different! It is the first step-by-step how-to book written especially for professional organizers, sharing not only tips, but the actual processes that will take your clients' spaces from disorganized messes to organized successes!

Now, if you're not a professional organizer, don't toss this book aside. You'll gain a lot out of reading it. You'll learn insider secrets that only the pros know, and you'll quickly realize that getting organized doesn't have to be complex or necessarily time consuming. (You'll even find some tips especially for non-pros scattered throughout the book!) Start out with one of the small spaces and see how it goes. If you discover organizing success, keep going with some larger spaces. If you are still struggling, it might be a sign that hiring a professional organizer would be helpful to you. You can find one near you by visiting the website of the National Association of Professional Organizers: www.napo.net.

No matter where you are on your organizing journey, I wish you happiness and success!

Sara ☺

Sara Pedersen, Professional Organizer

six steps to success

This book begins with techniques to organize small, simple spaces (like a drawer or linen closet), and then moves on to more complex projects (like a home office or kitchen). While some projects take more brain power, time, emotion, and physical stamina, all organizing spaces, big and small, can be made orderly by following these six manageable steps:

1. Assess & Plan
2. Empty, Quick-Toss & Sort
3. Declutter
4. Declare a Home
5. Contain & Label
6. Clean Up & Maintain

1. ASSESS & PLAN

An assessment (sometimes called a needs assessment) is a chance for a professional organizer to visit a person's home or office and give it an unbiased look. It's a time to ask lots of questions, do lots of listening, and then allow the client to hear the big picture plan for the project. It's an opportunity to break down the project into logical steps and roughly gauge how much time a project might take to complete. (Please note that detailed information about the assessment process can be found in the book *Born to Organize*, which details how to start up a professional organizing career.)

if you're not a pro

Even if you're a non-pro going it alone, the Assess & Plan stage is uber-important! You'll want to clearly define your goals for getting organized, figure out what has kept you from reaching your goals in the past, and make a plan to complete your organizing project.

Now is the time to discover:

• why the client wants to get organized — what are the ultimate goals?
• which spaces to organize, what they look like, and what they need
• the client's organizational challenges

Professional organizers can use the basic questions of "What is working well in this space?", "What is not working well in this space?", and "What things do you use most often?" Explore as you go and get more information as necessary.

Assessing the space to be organized involves taking a tour of the room(s) to be organized and possibly the entire home. Take notes while you walk and talk. Take measurements if helpful. Ask questions about how things come and go in the space. For example, if papers are piling up in the kitchen, you'll want to know what types of papers enter daily, who brings them in, and where they usually end up. You'll see patterns and habits develop. You'll also get a feel for the categories of stuff the clients own. What do they need daily vs. weekly vs. monthly vs. almost never?

What type of organizing products or tools do you see? Are they being used effectively? Do the clients need more/different organizing products? Do they prefer visible or hidden storage? Is their space used wisely or would the room(s) benefit from some space planning? Is the space big enough for the activities they want to do? What is the decorating style of the home (modern, country, contemporary, urban, etc.)?

As a professional organizer, you will be asking lots of questions during this step. For example, as you pick up an item, you'll often ask, "How do you use this?" or "When was the last time you used this?" And if you're reviewing current organizing systems, you might ask, "How does that work for you?" You'll be looking for habits, patterns, and dominant learning styles.

After you assess the space and situation, it's time to prioritize. What should you start with? Generally speaking, begin in the areas that are bothering the clients the most. But remember that all parts work as a whole. For example, if the pantry is driving a client nuts, that may be the starting point for the day. But remember that the pantry works in conjunction with any other food storage areas in the home.

Now that you're in the space, you'll have a better idea of timing. How much do you think you can accomplish today? What will you do on subsequent visits? Run it past the client and see if the schedule is satisfactory.

2. EMPTY, QUICK-TOSS & SORT

To begin any organizing project, designate a sorting area — clear some floor space or use a table, bed, or counter in the room. Then, item by item, remove each thing from its current spot and start sorting into logical categories. Each household is unique, so the categories will mirror the homeowner's lifestyles and priorities. What's important to them? What do they love to do? Create categories based on how they live (or want to live). Next, if there is a large volume of items, go a step further and create sub-categories. One great thing about sorting is that you'll easily see duplicate items, which will aid in the next step of decluttering. Some clients are great sorters and will jump right in. Others will struggle and need more direction in this area. Remember, you are teaching at all times, and so they are learning by observation. Don't just do it for them. Work alongside your clients.

Additionally, in many organizing projects, it's helpful to add a "quick-toss" to this phase, immediately tossing out items that are easily released before the sorting phase. If you see something obviously broken, stained, rusted, mildewed, unusable, or past its prime, now is the time to place it in the trash or, whenever possible, the recycling bin.

3. DECLUTTER

Essentially, this is the downsizing phase. In the previous step, you sorted everything into categories. Now you'll start decluttering. It will be helpful to have a few large boxes labeled "donate," "fix," and "relocate," plus some large trash and recycling bags. This is the stage where clients especially need support from professional organizers. If part of their goal is to declutter and downsize, the sorting phase will have shown them duplicate items. During this stage, a professional organizer can help them make decisions about whether to keep or toss. Try saying, "When was the last time you used this?" or "Do you really need four of these? Which is your favorite?" Those with emotional attachment and hoarding issues will have a difficult time with this stage. If your clients are *overly* sentimental about their stuff, try minimizing their physical contact with it. Allow clients to make the decisions, but help them realize that if they don't let go of some things, they won't reach their goal of decluttering or downsizing. As always, have that final goal in mind.

if you're not a pro

Research shows that once a person touches something, memories flood back and they're likely to want to keep it. You can help avoid these feelings by minimizing physical contact with your stuff. If you're overly sentimental, consider having a friend help by showing you items so you don't have to touch them.

4. DECLARE A HOME

When assigning "homes" for categories of items, think about where clients are most likely to use certain items and the frequency of use. Pull aside the things they use most often, and store them where they use them and in easy-to-access areas. Keeping similar things together will help your clients navigate the space more easily. Put infrequently used items way up high, down low, or in the back. Where do they usually leave specific things? That may be where the home needs to be, and by actually designating the spot as its home, it's more likely to work. "Declaring a Home" can mean deciding in which room a category of things should reside. It can also mean deciding which piece of furniture they go in or on (including the purchase of new storage items like shelving or cubbies, as necessary) or where the furniture should be placed (including some space planning and furniture rearrangement if necessary).

A note about doing these steps in the correct order: Sometimes it seems as though you should containerize first and then assign a home. But in most cases, you need to know where things will "live" before you can buy the correctly sized organizing containers.

5. CONTAIN & LABEL

By placing some similar items in containers within their homes, you'll make storage spaces look neat and retrieval easier. You won't be containerizing everything, of course. But there are some very helpful organizing products out there. You can bring along some basics yourself, use containers that your clients already own, or give them a shopping list. (Remember to take into account your clients' budgets and decorating styles that you learned during your assessments.) Be sure to make neat, easy-to-read labels for all containers so things return to their homes after each use. A label maker is a great tool for this task. Hanging or clip-on tags are an option for baskets or bins that don't have a smooth surface conducive to label-maker tape.

6. CLEAN UP & MAINTAIN

Once everything is in its proper place, now is a good time to take the trash and recycling out of the house. Load donations into a vehicle so they are out of the way, or call a local donation pick-up service. Grab the relocation box and help redistribute its contents to the appropriate rooms in the house, being careful not to get sidetracked into a new organizing project at that moment. (If you don't have the time or desire to help with the redistribution stage, it can be assigned as "homework" for the client to do later that day.)

if you're not a pro

No home is ever going to maintain itself. After you complete step #5, you absolutely must create a plan to maintain an organized space. That means figuring out how often you need to do quick tidy-ups (daily or weekly) and some deep-cleaning (often quarterly or semi-annually.)

This is also the time to discuss how this newly organized space will stay that way. Maintenance shouldn't take a lot of time, but it needs to be done planfully and with intention on a regular basis.

The way you'll hone your organizing techniques is to practice, practice, practice! You'll discover what works best for many of your typical organizing scenarios. But, before you get started on any organizing job, you'll need to do an assessment of the space and situation, followed by some goal-making and planning! Keep reading to see how this six-step process works in a variety of household spaces.

before you start

Each section of this book begins with a list of storage examples for that type of space. For instance, the "organize an entryway" examples show that this space can take many forms, from a closet or mudroom to other options like a bench with interior storage, a coat rack or wall hooks, and/or a table with storage baskets underneath. This will allow you to think outside the box a bit and see that each home's organizing potential is unique.

Following that, you'll find a list of basic supplies needed. Please note that this section doesn't delve into specific supplies, but you will find a list of storage container recommendations in the sidebar of most sections. Just remember that each organizing space and situation is unique and it is up to you to find what works best for your client's space, budget, and aesthetic preferences. At the end of this book, you'll find lists and sketches of organizing tools that may be helpful to you as you organize a home. These all-purpose tools could be used in a variety of organizing scenarios.

Next, you'll find the time commitment for each project. This is a rough estimate of hours it might take to complete this task. Remember, this is only a guide. Your job may take less or more time, depending upon decision-making ability, speed, endurance, enthusiasm, and the amount of stuff in the space. These estimates do not apply to hoarding situations.

Then, you'll delve into the six steps described in the previous section. Each sidebar lists some potential goals for the space. (Remember, the secret to organizing success is to know why someone wants to get organized in the first place!) You'll also find a "quick-toss list" in the sidebar that gives permission to immediately toss things that are in rough shape.

Whether you're a new professional organizer just testing the waters, an experienced organizer who wants to brush up or learn some new techniques, or a homeowner who wants to try refreshing a space like a pro, these steps will break down the process so it's easy to understand and implement.

if you're not a pro

The time estimates listed apply to people who are working with a professional organizer. But if you're someone with good follow-through and quick decision-making skills, you may be able to complete tasks within a similar timeline as those working with a pro.

organizing
small, simple
spaces

Small spaces have the
potential for big messes.
However, with just a little
bit of organizing know-how,
you can transform them from
disastrous to delightful.

Organize a
DRAWER

EXAMPLES OF STORAGE
- kitchen drawer
- junk drawer
- dresser drawer
- bathroom drawer
- desk drawer

SUPPLIES NEEDED
- trash bags/recycling bin, donation box, relocation box
- spray cleaner and cleaning cloth
- drawer dividers/boxes
- drawer liners or contact paper, if desired
- label maker

TIME COMMITMENT
- 15–30 minutes

1. ASSESS & PLAN
Drawers make great inspirational, quickie projects. Generally, a drawer can be organized in less than 30 minutes, so they give a boost of satisfaction and confidence. To get started, simply ask, "What is the purpose of this drawer?" and "What type of items should live within it?"

2. EMPTY, QUICK-TOSS & SORT
Empty out everything from the drawer by placing all items on a nearby counter or table. Check the quick-toss list to see what can be placed immediately into the trash. Wipe down the drawer so it's a clean slate. (This is a good time to put down drawer liners or contact paper if you're so inclined.)

Now, sort everything into categories. For example, if you're sorting a junk drawer, you might have categories of office supplies, fix-it supplies, keys, buttons, batteries, etc. If you're sorting a bathroom drawer, you might have categories of make-up, teeth cleaning, first aid, etc. A desk drawer might have paper clips, push pins, rubber bands, staples, binder clips, sticky note pads, pens, pencils, etc. A dresser drawer

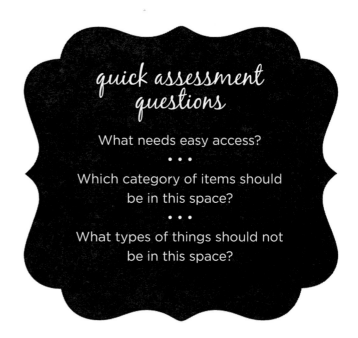

quick assessment questions

What needs easy access?

• • •

Which category of items should be in this space?

• • •

What types of things should not be in this space?

potential goals for this space

quickly and easily find what is needed

reduce clutter

have a clear definition of what this drawer should hold

corral a drawer's contents with containers

ensure that items get returned to the proper place

might have socks and underwear, etc.

3. DECLUTTER
Then, look at the remaining piles and recognize duplicate items. Ask if multiples could be pared down. Place items that are no longer loved or needed into the donation box.

4. DECLARE A HOME
If you find anything that would be better off in another area of the home, place it in the relocation box for redistribution at the end of the project. For everything that is staying in the drawer, move on to the next step, since the home has already been declared as the drawer you are working on.

5. CONTAIN & LABEL
Now that you can clearly see categories and all the keepers, decide on the type and size of containers you'll need. There are many types of drawer organizers available. One option is a plastic cutlery tray that you find in the kitchen section of a home goods store like Target. Or, for more customizable products, check your local organizing stores or online. You'll find inserts that you can expand or even cut/snap to the exact size and shape you need. Another option is to configure small boxes to organize the space. You can find lovely lucite or bamboo boxes at organizing stores, or you can save money by using boxes already on hand at home, such as checkbook boxes, mint tins, plastic berry crates, or any other little containers you find. For a pretty aesthetic, you could cover any recycled boxes with colored or patterned scrapbooking, contact, or wrapping paper.

Place items in appropriately sized containers and decide if you need lids on any containers. (Usually lids are not needed on containers that are inside drawers, because it adds one step to the maintenance process, but if items will spill out without a lid, use one.) Finally, label each container or tray section using a label maker.

6. CLEAN UP & MAINTAIN
Put the donation box in the car or near the exit so it leaves the home immediately. Take out the trash. Grab the relocation box and redistribute all of its contents appropriately. Plan to give this drawer a tweak every couple months to keep it neat.

quick-toss list

pens that don't work

stubby pencils

broken crayons

scraps of paper

unimportant receipts

unidentifiable keys

dead batteries

expired medications

old make-up

stained/ripped clothing

Organize an ENTRYWAY

EXAMPLES OF STORAGE
- entryway closet
- mudroom
- storage bench
- cubbies or wall-mounted shelves
- bench or table with baskets underneath
- hooks, hook rail, or coat rack

SUPPLIES NEEDED
- trash can, donation box, relocation box, fix-it box
- spray cleaner and cleaning cloth
- broom and dust pan
- storage containers
- label maker and/or tags to hang from containers/baskets

TIME COMMITMENT
- 1–3 hours

1. ASSESS & PLAN

First impressions are important, and the entryway is the first thing to greet homeowners and their guests. It needs to be both functional and inviting, providing a spot to drop keys, bags, and coats upon arrival in the home. But if it's not organized, it's easy for this small space to become cluttered and unused.

Decide what should reside in the entryway. Ideally, this should be a spot for coats and other outerwear, umbrellas, daily-used backpacks, purses, briefcases, and totes — anything needing easy access on the way out the door. Don't let the entryway become a catch-all for things you don't know what to do with.

It also needs a dedicated space to drop things that need to leave the house — a "launching pad."

quick assessment questions

What gets dropped on the floor as family members come home?

• • •

What do you frequently forget as you leave the house?

• • •

What types of things should not be in this space?

potential goals for this space

make it easy to get out the door on time

create a good first impression for guests

have only in-season clothing in the space

have a place to sit while putting on shoes

have a place for kids to hang backpacks

have a place to drop keys and cell phone

2. EMPTY, QUICK-TOSS & SORT

Empty out everything from the space by placing all items on a nearby counter, table, or floor. Check the quick-toss list to see what can be placed immediately into the trash can. Sweep out the space and wipe down any shelves.

Now, sort everything into categories: cold-weather coats, warm-weather jackets, mittens and gloves, hats, baseball caps, umbrellas, tote bags, purses, backpacks, boots, shoes, etc. Now, do a second-level sort of clothing items by family member.

3. DECLUTTER

High-quality outerwear with broken zippers or small rips can be placed in the fix-it box, the trash, or the donation box as appropriate. Then, look at the remaining category piles and recognize duplicate items. Ask if multiples could be pared down. Check sizes of coats, boots, and shoes and put those that no longer fit into the donation box. Place items that are no longer loved or needed into the donation box.

4. DECLARE A HOME

Now, begin to maximize the space. If the entryway has a closet, reevaluate its set-up. If it has a single rod across the top, could you raise it a bit and add a second rod below to double the hanging space? Could shelves be added above the rod or run across the depth of the closet? Could you add a tiered shoe rack on the floor? Maximize every inch of space! While you're at it, invest in sturdy wooden hangers so coats hang neatly. Also consider if a chair or bench is needed in this space to aid when slipping on shoes and boots.

Also consider space outside the closet. This is especially necessary if there is no closet or if it's very small. For example, a coat rack or set of wall-mounted hooks in the entryway will work wonders if closet space is minimal. A sturdy hook rail (mounted into the wall's studs) creates an easy way for kids to hang backpacks and jackets.

If you find anything that would be better off in another area of the home, place it into the relocation box for redistribution at the end of the project. For everything that is staying in the entryway, move on to the next step.

quick-toss list

broken umbrellas

gloves/mittens without mates

anything broken

anything ripped

anything stained

dry cleaner hangers and plastic bags

5. CONTAIN & LABEL

Use containers to corral the keepers. This not only makes the space looks neater, but it also helps quickly find what is needed. For example, a pretty urn can hold umbrellas, a bench with storage under the seat can hold outerwear, and a wicker basket on the floor can hold shoes. Label baskets or boxes on the shelves for other out-the-door items, such as mittens, hats, and dog leashes. Hanging sweater bags or hanging shoe racks can hold not only shoes, but other out-the-door necessities. Corral sports equipment in large baskets or tote bags hanging from sturdy hooks.

6. CLEAN UP & MAINTAIN

Put the donation box in the car or near the exit so it leaves the home immediately. Take out the trash. Grab the relocation box and redistribute all of its contents appropriately.

Finally, set up an out-the-door launching pad. Dedicate one basket near the door for items that need to leave the house, such as library books and DVDs to be returned, dry cleaning to be dropped off, and things to be delivered to family or friends.

Plan to give the entryway a tweak at the beginning of each season to keep it neat and filled with weather-appropriate outerwear.

storage containers

bins/boxes/baskets that are open-top

bins/boxes/baskets with lids

cubby organizers, large or small

double hang closet rods

hanging sweater bags

hooks, hookrails, over-the-door racks

key rack

rolling or storage carts/chests

shoe storage: floor racks, hanging shoe racks, shoe trees, shoe cubbies

umbrella stands or urns

wooden hangers

Organize a
LINEN CLOSET

EXAMPLES OF STORAGE
- closet
- cupboard
- chest of drawers, trunk, or armoire
- shelving unit
- underbed storage

SUPPLIES NEEDED
- trash can, donation box, relocation box
- spray cleaner and cleaning cloth
- broom and dust pan and/or vacuum
- storage containers
- label maker and/or tags to hang from containers/baskets

TIME COMMITMENT
- 1–3 hours

1. ASSESS & PLAN
There is usually not a lot of sentimental attachment to a linen closet's contents, so this quick and easy project brings immediate gratification. Whether you're organizing an actual linen closet, or a makeshift linen storage space like a dresser, cupboard in the bathroom, or some space under a bed, it's important to keep it neat and easily identifiable. Determine what types of items should live in this space. Will it be storage for sheet sets, blankets, towels, overflow toilet paper, cleaning supplies, and/or miscellaneous health and beauty supplies?

2. EMPTY, QUICK-TOSS & SORT
Empty out everything from the space by placing all items on a nearby counter, table, or floor. (If linens are stored in multiple areas of the home, be sure to gather all linens together now. This includes all sheet sets and bathroom towels (with the exception of towel sets that are only used and stored in a particular bathroom, such as a lower-level powder room). That way, you can easily see everything at once. Check the quick-toss list to see what can be placed immediately into

quick assessment questions

What types of things are currently housed in this space?

• • •

What types of things should not be in this space?

• • •

How many sheet and towels sets should be kept?

potential goals for this space

make it easy to find the right size of sheets

have easy access to fresh towels

store overflow bathroom supplies

have it not be a dumping ground for miscellaneous items

the trash. Wipe down the shelves and/or sweep or vacuum the floor so it's a clean slate.

Now, sort everything into categories, such as towels, sheets, blankets, and pillows. You might also find bathroom necessities, such as cleaning supplies, paper products, and medications. That's okay, but remember that the linen closet should not be a catch-all!

3. DECLUTTER

Once you can see your categories, consider the quantities and begin to downsize. See if you can narrow down the sheet sets to two per bed (one on the bed, and one in the closet). Donate old, ratty towels to a local animal shelter. Get rid of extra blankets and pillows that are no longer used.

4. DECLARE A HOME

If you find anything that would be better off in another area of the home, place it into the relocation box for redistribution at the end of the project.

Next, begin returning items to the closet, cupboard, dresser, or underbed storage. Think carefully about proper placement. It is key! Store bulky items that are used infrequently (such as beach towels or heavy blankets) on the very top shelf or, if there is no linen closet, consider placing them into space-saving vacuum storage bags or plastic storage boxes under a bed or on a top shelf of a bedroom closet, or fold them neatly inside a trunk. To keep piles from toppling over, consider shelf dividers which slip onto shelves.

Place items used most often at eye level so they can be easily reached. Fold towels neatly and store either by size or set. Or, roll the towels for an eye-pleasing, easy-to-grab storage method. Decide if all towels should be in one centralized location, such as the linen closet, or if it makes more sense to put specific sets within each bathroom. Sheets can be stored in a linen closet or cupboard. Sometimes, it makes sense to store specific sets in the bedroom for which they are intended.

quick-toss list

ripped or faded towels

ripped or faded sheets

cartoon character sheets or blankets (if kids are grown)

too-flat pillows

expired medications

past-their-prime beauty products

5. CONTAIN & LABEL

Sheets sets can be slipped into their coordinating pillowcases for easy retrieval, stacking similar sizes in the same row. Or, tie a ribbon around each folded set for grab and go convenience, noting the size on the ribbon. If storing bathroom essentials in the linen closet, be sure to contain them in pretty boxes or baskets. A hanging overdoor shoe bag is another way to corral smaller items, utilizing the space on the back of a closet door. Stash bathroom cleaning products in a handled tote for easy grab and go on cleaning day.

Finally, be sure to label the shelves and containers so that items return to their correct homes, ensuring an organized linen closet for years to come.

6. CLEAN UP

Put the donation box in the car or near the exit so it leaves the home immediately. Take out the trash. Grab the relocation box and redistribute all of its contents appropriately.

Make a plan to maintain the linen closet on a semi-annual basis. Each spring and fall makes sense, because families are often changing out warm-weather blankets and sheets for cold-weather ones.

storage containers

bins/boxes/baskets that are open-top

bins/boxes/baskets with lids

hanging overdoor shoe bags

stacking bins

shelf dividers

undershelf baskets

vacuum "space" bags

Organize a
BATHROOM

EXAMPLES OF STORAGE
- containers or pull-outs under the sink
- containers on countertop
- hooks on back of door
- bathroom cupboard
- shelving or rack above toilet
- medicine cabinet

SUPPLIES NEEDED
- trash bags/recycling bin, donation box, relocation box
- spray cleaner and cleaning cloth
- broom and dust pan
- storage containers
- label maker and/or tags to hang from containers/baskets
- drawer liners or contact paper, if desired

TIME COMMITMENT
- 2–4 hours

1. ASSESS & PLAN
A bathroom is the smallest, but often busiest, room in the house. Your job is to figure out what needs to be done to make it function more smoothly. Do make-up supplies need to be downsized? Is it easy to locate a new bottle of shampoo when the old one is empty? Determine what types of things need to be kept close at hand and what could be stored out of the way (perhaps even in another room).

2. EMPTY, QUICK-TOSS & SORT
Empty out everything from all drawers and cupboards and place all items on the floor. Check the quick-toss list to see what can be placed immediately into the trash. (Be sure to dispose of medications appropriately.) Wipe down all drawers and cupboards so they are a clean slate. (This is a good time to put down drawer liners or contact paper if you're so inclined.) Sort into categories, such as first aid, hair care, body cleansers, shaving, tooth care, cosmetics, paper products, and cleaning supplies.

quick assessment questions

How many people use this space on a daily basis?

• • •

Do you store things in here that should really go elsewhere?

• • •

How many of the beauty supplies are really being used?

potential goals for this space

make the countertop more attractive by reducing clutter

maximize storage space

make it easier & quicker to clean

create a personal tote for each family member's bathroom necessities

avoid over-buying cleaning products

3. DECLUTTER

Once everything is grouped together, you'll see where there are duplicates. A bunch of past-their-prime hand towels could be replaced with a couple of fresh, new sets. Those collections of miniature-sized hotel shampoos could be donated to a local homeless or women's shelter. Now is also the time to toss anything that hasn't been used in the past year. For example, if curly hair is out and straight hair is in, maybe it's time to donate the curling irons.

4. DECLARE A HOME

If you find anything that would be better off in another area of the home, place it into the relocation box for redistribution at the end of the project.

Some things in a bathroom are shared items, while others may belong to a specific person. Take into account the available space in the medicine cabinet, vanity drawers, and under-sink storage, as well as in the linen closet. If you need to add storage, consider installing shelving on a wall or a free-standing cabinet above the toilet.

Keep the bathroom safe for little ones by storing medications and bathroom cleaning products out of their reach. (Many medications lose effectiveness in the bathroom humidity, so consider storing them in another room.)

5. CONTAIN & LABEL

Now that you can clearly see categories and all the keepers, decide on the type and size of containers you'll need. As you place items, group them into their categories, and/or assign a specific place for each member of the household. For example, each person could have one drawer, one basket on the shelf, or one toteable caddy. Countertop clutter can be kept at bay by using attractive containers to corral categories of items.

quick-toss list

expired medications

expired sunscreens

past-their-prime cosmetics

ripped or faded towels

ripped or faded sheets

If you're grouping by category, you could use baskets, bins, or specific areas on the shelves for easy locating. Be sure to label so that everyone in the household knows how to find necessities. If towel bars are in short supply, add hooks behind the door or on the wall so everyone has a place to hang towels. An under-the-sink, two-tier sliding organizer could be perfect for cleaning supplies.

Finally, label each container or tray section using a label maker or tags.

6. CLEAN UP & MAINTAIN

Put the donation box in the car or near the exit so it leaves the home immediately. Take out the trash. Grab the relocation box and redistribute all of its contents appropriately.

Make a plan to weed through medications and make-up twice annually, tossing anything expired or outdated. At this time, donate ratty towels to a local animal shelter and remove anything that has found its way into the bathroom that doesn't belong there.

storage containers

bins/boxes/baskets that are open-top

bins/boxes/baskets with lids

cleaning caddies

drawer dividers

hooks, hook rails, over-the-door racks

laundry baskets and/or sorting hampers

shelf dividers

stackable bins

turntable

undersink pull-out baskets

undersink, two-tier sliding organizers

Organize a
LAUNDRY ROOM

EXAMPLES OF STORAGE
- cupboard above washer/dryer
- shelves over or alongside washer/dryer
- cabinet next to washer/dryer
- slim rolling cart between washer/dryer
- long folding table with baskets underneath

SUPPLIES NEEDED
- trash can, donation box, relocation box
- spray cleaner and cleaning cloth
- broom and dust pan
- storage containers
- label maker and/or tags to hang from containers/baskets

TIME COMMITMENT
- 1–3 hours (not including doing any piled-up laundry)

1. ASSESS & PLAN

A laundry room's functionality can greatly affect a home owner's ability to process laundry from the in-the-hamper stage to the neat-and-folded-in-the-drawer phase. The goal should be to have this space be a drive-thru for clothing, not a long-term parking space. Dirty clothing in and out in the same day should be the plan! Also, consider any other categories of things that are in this space, such as cleaning supplies and utility items like light bulbs and batteries.

2. EMPTY, QUICK-TOSS & SORT

First, if there are piles of dirty laundry, they need to removed from the space. (Ideally, it would be best to have all clothing laundered before you begin this project, but if not, at least clear them out so you have a blank slate.) Then, empty out everything from all cabinets and place all items on a nearby counter, table, or floor. Check the quick-toss list to see what can be placed immediately into the trash. Wipe down any shelving so it's a clean slate. (This is a good time to put down drawer liners or contact paper, if you're so inclined.) Now, sort everything into categories, such as laundry cleaning supplies, home cleaning supplies, hangers, etc.

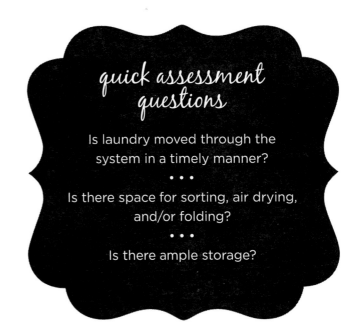

quick assessment questions

Is laundry moved through the system in a timely manner?

• • •

Is there space for sorting, air drying, and/or folding?

• • •

Is there ample storage?

potential goals for this space

create a space to sort, wash, dry, fold, and iron clothing

have a place to air-dry clothing

have laundry sorted before it gets to the laundry room

have a flat surface to fold laundry

have cleaning supplies easily accessible

3. DECLUTTER

Then, look at the remaining piles and recognize duplicate items. Ask if multiples could be pared down. Place items that are no longer loved or needed into the donation box.

4. DECLARE A HOME

If you find anything that would be better off in another area of the home, place it in the relocation box for redistribution at the end of the project. If you need more storage space, add a couple of rows of shelving above the washer/dryer. If hidden storage is preferred, install some inexpensive cabinets (available at any home improvement store) on one wall or assemble a free-standing cabinet. Other things to consider adding in a laundry room are a pull-out air-drying rack and a rod on which to hang clothing on hangers after being pulled from the dryer. And don't forget to use wall space — hang the broom and mop from hooks. Install a wall mount ironing board holder to keep the ironing board off the floor. Remember to keep cleaners and chemicals out of reach of small children.

5. CONTAIN & LABEL

Now that you can clearly see categories and all the keepers, decide on the type and size of containers. Use baskets and boxes (labeled, of course) to hold not-as-frequently used things such as clothespins, old rags, and a pile of missing-a-mate socks. Keep laundry necessities — such as detergent, stain removal pens, fabric softener, an iron, starch, and bleach — within easy reach for grab and go convenience. (Consider using a turntable to hold cleaning supplies for easy access.) Finally, label each container or tray section using a label maker or tags.

6. CLEAN UP & MAINTAIN

Put the donation box in the car or near the exit so it leaves the home immediately. Take out the trash. Grab the relocation box and redistribute all of its contents appropriately.

Make a plan to give the laundry room a quick-tidy once a month, and create a plan to keep laundry under control at all times.

quick-toss list

clothing beyond repair

overabundance of cleaning supplies

dry-cleaner wire hangers and any excess of other hangers

storage containers

bins/boxes/baskets that are open-top

bins/boxes/baskets with lids

cleaning caddies

drying rack

hooks or hookrail

laundry baskets and/or sorting hampers

rolling cart

stacking shelves

turntable

wall mount ironing board holder

organizing complex projects

These rooms are fun to tackle,
and they have the added element
of space planning. In this section,
you'll learn how to organize
the bedroom, clothing, toy area,
living area, kitchen,
storage areas, and craft room.
In addition, you'll learn
how to eco-organize!

Organize a
BEDROOM

EXAMPLES OF STORAGE
- dresser or armoire
- closet
- nightstand
- underbed storage
- trunk or storage ottoman

SUPPLIES NEEDED
- trash bags/recycling bin, donation box, relocation box, fix-it box
- spray cleaner and cleaning cloth
- broom and dust pan and/or vacuum
- storage containers
- label maker and/or tags to hang from containers/baskets

TIME COMMITMENT
- 3–6 hours (not including clothing organization)

1. ASSESS & PLAN
The bedroom should be a place of peace and relaxation. Clutter in a bedroom is a big no-no! Yet many people fall into bed each evening with clothing draped over chairs and piles of clutter toppling over, and then wonder why they aren't getting a good night's sleep. As you create a plan, figure out what types of clutter are in the room, why it is accumulating in the space, and what you could do to remove, reduce, or reroute it.

(Please note that clothing storage is addressed later in this book separately because it is a complex topic, so you can reference that section in tandem with this one. You will want to tackle all the clothing at one time, and perhaps work on the other non-clothing items at another time.)

quick assessment questions

Does this room promote good sleep and relaxation? If not, why not?

• • •

What types of things should be removed from this space?

• • •

Is there enough appropriate storage in this space?

potential goals for this space

have a relaxing place to read and sleep

be able to get dressed quickly and efficiently each morning

create a more beautiful, clutter-free space

have a small desk area for writing

2. EMPTY, SORT & QUICK-TOSS

Start by removing everything from all flat surfaces, such as the tops of dressers, nightstands, and tables. Clear out all non-clothing items from inside any furniture, such as drawers, armoires, trunks, or nightstands. Place all items on the bed or floor. That way, you can easily see everything at once. Check the quick-toss list to see what can be placed immediately into the trash/recycling bin. Wipe down the surfaces.

Now, sort everything into categories. Some categories might include books and magazines, spare change, jewelry, paperwork, memorabilia, DVDs and CDs, exercise equipment, etc.

3. DECLUTTER

Once you can see your categories, consider the quantities, and begin to downsize. Now is the time to get rid of things that don't promote relaxation in the bedroom, such as the treadmill or possibly, the computer or television. Paperwork is also a no-no in this space.

4. DECLARE A HOME

If you find anything that would be better off in another area of the home, place it into the relocation box for redistribution at the end of the project.

Next, think about where categories of things should live for ease of use. Should the books and magazines go near the bed, or would they be more convenient next to a reading chair? What items are needed on top of a bedside table or nightstand? Things that are not used frequently might be able to be stored under the bed or in a trunk at the foot of the bed.

Now is also the time to do a little space planning. The bed would be best placed on the room's longest wall or opposite the door entry. Nightstands or small tables should flank the bed, with small lamps or wall-mounted swing-lamps. A dresser could go directly across from the bed or on the second longest wall. If the family likes to curl up with a book, add a cozy chair and floor lamp in one corner.

quick-toss list

old magazines

old receipts

unnecessary paperwork and accumulated mail

ratty bed linens

old blankets

too-flat pillows

anything broken

exercise equipment that is in poor shape or never used

Although paperwork really doesn't belong in the bedroom, if it must reside there, then create a plan to corral it in an out-of-sight manner. A narrow writing desk or secretary would be an appropriate addition for someone who wants to pay bills and review paperwork in the bedroom or for the budding author.

5. CONTAIN & LABEL

Clutter should be out of sight in a bedroom. Corral bedside reading material in an attractive basket or magazine rack. Consider baskets or boxes that match the room's decor to hold specific categories of things. Purchase underbed storage boxes to keep non-essential items out of sight. Then, label containers with a label maker or tags that can hang from baskets.

6. CLEAN UP & MAINTAIN

Put the donation box in the car or near the exit so it leaves the home immediately. Take out the trash. Grab the relocation box and redistribute all of its contents appropriately.

Make a plan to tidy the bedroom daily, and to schedule an organizing maintenance session quarterly.

This project may be preceded or followed by the clothing organization steps found in the next section of this book.

storage containers

boxes/baskets/bins that are attractive enough to be displayed (fabric, wicker, leather, etc.)

drawer dividers

magazine rack

multimedia boxes

trash can

underbed storage boxes

vacuum-sealed "space bags"

Organize
CLOTHING

EXAMPLES OF STORAGE
- bedroom closet (walk-in or standard)
- dresser
- armoire
- underbed storage boxes
- trunk or storage ottoman
- nightstand

SUPPLIES NEEDED
- trash bags/recycling bin, donation box, relocation box, fix-it box
- spray cleaner and cleaning cloth
- broom and dust pan and/or vacuum
- storage containers
- label maker and/or tags to hang from containers/baskets

TIME COMMITMENT
- 4–10 hours

1. ASSESS & PLAN

Organizing a clothing collection is one of the most satisfying clean-up projects you can tackle. But without planning, its sheer enormity can leave you with more chaos than before you started. Your goal is to come up with a system that will maximize the space, time, and wardrobe and allow for easy maintenance. While most clothing resides in a closet, it must work in conjunction with other storage spaces outside the closet, such as a dresser or armoire.

Before you start, if space is limited, make a plan to keep only the "A" team or current clothes in the closet. Shift seasonal clothes, maternity, and "other size" items to another storage space, such as under the bed or in the basement. Many people can reduce the amount of clothing in their closet by half if they follow this guideline.

quick assessment questions

What are the main categories of clothing?

• • •

What items could be placed in off-season storage?

• • •

What types of things need quick and instant access?

potential goals for this space

make getting ready in the morning a snap

make it easier to put away clothing in the evening and on laundry day

get rid of clothing that no longer fits

create a new wardrobe

make the closet visually appealing

2. EMPTY, SORT & QUICK-TOSS

Make space to spread everything out. (A bed works great for this.) You'll be taking out every item in the closet, dresser drawers, and anything else that contains clothing.

As you take things out, check the quick-toss list to see what can be placed immediately into the trash. Because of the sheer enormity of some people's clothing collections, it is okay to start the declutter phase in tandem with the empty-ing phase. If something triggers an immediate "toss it!" reaction, it's okay to place it into the donation box right away.

As you sort, separate into work and casual wear by item type, then group similar items by color. Button-down shirts, dress pants, blazers, dresses, skirts, etc. should all be batched together so you can quickly see what you have and assess its placement. Make a separate pile for each category of casual clothing, such as pants, t-shirts, shorts, yoga/sweat-pants, and sweatshirts. Also group together shoes, belts, and accessories.

Once the closet is empty, give it a good vacuuming and dusting, and wipe down any shelves in the closet and inside drawers.

3. DECLUTTER

Take a look at the category piles and consider the quantities as you begin to downsize. For each item, ask whether it's been used/worn in the past year. Knowing that we wear only about 20 percent of our clothes 80 percent of the time will aid the letting go process. Also note that over-stuffed drawers are the likely culprit when clean laundry doesn't get put away. It simply takes too much effort to jam everything in, so make a goal to only fill drawers about two-thirds full.

If you find anything that would be better off in another area of the home, place it into the relocation box for redistribution at the end of the project. Also keep on hand the fix-it box (for items that need repairing) and the donation box.

quick-toss list

any clothing that is stained or ripped

shoes that are past their prime

clothing left over from the high school years (unless, of course, you're still in high school)

souvenir t-shirts

broken jewelry

socks without mates

underwear that has lost its elasticity

dry-cleaner hangers and plastic bags

4. DECLARE A HOME

Now that you can see what you actually have, start measuring. How much of the clothing can realistically fit in the closet? If it only has one rod across the top, you may want to consider redesigning the closet for maximum space efficiency. Or, simple, inexpensive modifications can be made by adding a double hang closet rod to double the hanging space. You may also be able to adjust shelves and rods to better accommodate space needs.

Now, decide where each category of clothing will live. Remember, the closet works in tandem with any dressers, armoires, and underbed storage in the bedroom. Assign each item a home. Designate a shelf, section of rod, drawer, or container for each category of clothing. Come up with a system that will allow low maintenance of the decluttered space.

Section garments by type, then by color, so it's easy to see what's there. Hang pants, blazers, button-front shirts, dresses, and skirts. Fold t-shirts, tanks, sweaters, nightwear, swim wear, shorts, sweatshirts, sweatpants, and yoga pants. Don't put matching tops and bottoms together; this makes it difficult to see other ways to combine them. Arrange clothes so those that are worn most often are nearest the front of the closet.

During this stage, you might encourage a little more purging. Once you have everything sorted and stored, you may discover multiples of the same item. This is one last chance to get rid of those items that don't fit, are out of style, or are not practical. Remember, it's important to let clothing have a little breathing room to keep it wrinkle-free, as well as to allow easy viewing of a closet's contents.

5. CONTAIN & LABEL

While most clothing items will be hung in the closet or folded neatly in a dresser, storage containers or racks that are sturdy and sized appropriately will be helpful for smaller items like accessories and shoes. Sweaters, T-shirts, and sweatshirts line up nicely on shelves with the help of vertical shelf dividers or can be placed in clear plastic boxes or hanging canvas shelves. Accessories such as purses, scarves, and belts can be placed in clear boxes or attractive wicker baskets on open shelves.

storage containers

bins/boxes/baskets that are open-top

bins/boxes/baskets with lids

double hang closet rods

drawer dividers

hangers: wooden, velvet/no-slip, tube, pants, padded

hanging sweater bags

hanging overdoor shoe bags

hooks, hook rails, over-the-door racks

laundry baskets and/or sorting hampers

plastic stacking drawers

shelf dividers

shoe storage: floor rack, hanging shoe rack, shoe tree, shoe cubbies

vacuum-sealed "space bags"

It's helpful to standardize the hangers. Wooden, padded, tube, pants, or "huggable" velvet hangers, rather than cheap wire ones, will keep clothing in top-notch shape and avoid tangles. It's okay to use more than one kind of hanger to help clothing keep its shape. For example, padded hangers should be used for any hanging sweaters, but other kinds of shirts would be fine with tube or huggable hangers. Just keep them consistent in each section of the closet. And always hang clothes in the same direction. This will help reduce visual clutter and allow you to review your clothes at a glance.

For shoes, there are a multitude of storage options. Inexpensive clear plastic shoe boxes keep shoes dust-free and easily viewed. Or use overdoor shoe bags, hanging canvas shoe bags, or a neat tiered shoe rack or shoe tree on the floor.

Make sure to use ALL closet space. Underneath short-hanging garments, place a low trunk full of sweaters, a set of plastic drawers, or a simple wooden dresser filled with lingerie, swimsuits, and socks.

6. CLEAN UP & MAINTAIN

Put the donation boxes in the car or near the exit so they leave the home immediately. Take out the trash. Grab the relocation box and redistribute all of its contents appropriately. Review the contents of the fix-it box and determine if the cost of the repairs is worth saving the items. If so, make a plan to get them to the tailor shop this week. If not, they should go into the donation box.

Get rid of extra hangers, which just take up space. See if your local dry cleaner can recycle any unneeded wire hangers. Be sure to include a laundry hamper or basket in the closet or bedroom to make daily clean-up a snap.

Before you consider this job done, add a giveaway box to the closet to make donating easier. Make a plan to maintain this space on a semi-annual basis. In early spring and late fall, take a couple hours to switch out cold weather and warm weather clothing. Pull out anything that is dated or is simply never worn or loved, and put it into the donation box.

Organize a
TOY AREA

EXAMPLES OF STORAGE
- toy room
- corner of living/family room
- bedroom
- closet

SUPPLIES NEEDED
- trash bags/recycling bin, donation box, relocation box, fix-it box
- spray cleaner and cleaning cloth
- broom and dust pan and/or vacuum
- storage containers
- label maker and/or tags to hang from containers/baskets

TIME COMMITMENT
- 3–9 hours

1. ASSESS & PLAN

If a family is fortunate enough to have a dedicated space for their childrens' toys, it's likely they want advice on creating new storage methods to make the space look neater and more aesthetically appealing. It might be a dedicated toy or play room, just a corner of the living room, or an area of a kids' bedroom, but no matter the size, storage is a huge part of toy organization. Determine if new storage items need to be purchased (both containers and storage furniture), make recommendations, and get that into motion immediately.

Parents also look for ways to make clean-up time easier. In addition to creating kid-friendly storage solutions, building clean-up routines is essential to success. Families need to make organizing a part of each day. It's important to teach kids that every item they own has a "home" where it needs to return when they're done using it. Let kids know that they need to be responsible for their own possessions. Suggest a 10-minute clean-up every night before bedtime to keep a toy area tidy.

quick assessment questions

Are you satisfied with the amount of toys in the space?

• • •

What would you ideally like this space to look like?

• • •

How is toy clean-up time going?

potential goals for this space

make it easier for kids to find toys

make clean-up time easier

create a neater appearance to a chaotic space

corral and hide toys in a grown-up living space

2. EMPTY, SORT & QUICK-TOSS

Starting in one corner of the room, empty current storage bins and sort toys into categories. Check the quick-toss list to see what can be placed immediately into the trash/recycling bin. Create categories, such as puzzles and games, dolls, books, sports, dress-up, cars (large and small), blocks, videos and gaming, etc. Wipe down the shelves and/or sweep or vacuum the floor so it's a clean slate.

3. DECLUTTER

Once you can see your categories, consider the quantities, and begin to downsize. Often, the sheer volume of stuff in a kid's life — toys, sporting equipment, books, collections — is overwhelming. Most kids would be just as happy with less stuff. If kids are involved in the process, talk about how great it feels to donate to a local homeless shelter or a favorite charity.

4. DECLARE A HOME

If you find anything that would be better off in another area of the home, place it into the relocation box for redistribution at the end of the project.

Now, decide on zones for different types of play. Look at your categories, and figure out where they should reside within the space and what type of storage is needed. For example, look at the quantity of books being kept, and recommend appropriately sized bookshelves or bins. Large cubbies allow easy access to toys, yet keep a space from looking cluttered when combined with square fabric bins that fit the cubbies.

Sometimes, furniture can be found in other areas of the home. For example, an old armoire from a bedroom might be perfect to hold board games or to create an art supply station. The trunk left over from camp or college days might fit the bill for sports equipment or monster trucks.

5. CONTAIN & LABEL

Select containers that are easy for kids to open and close. Baskets or boxes without lids make clean-up easier than those with lids. (But sometimes lids are necessary to keep items from popping out, or to allow for stacking.)

quick-toss list

broken toys

puzzles missing pieces

games missing pieces

dried-out art supplies

scraps of paper

old VHS tapes

old cassette tapes

toys that are outgrown or no longer relevant

storage containers

bins/boxes/baskets that are open-top

boxes, clear plastic, with lids

cubby organizers, large or small

hanging overdoor shoe bags

rolling or storage carts/chests

stacking bins

turntables

Keep scale in mind. Small toys would get lost inside the ubiquitous toy chest, but larger toys like trucks or dress-up clothes might be perfect there. Smaller items like Barbie clothing or Polly Pockets might be better off in small, clear plastic boxes with lids for easy portability. Or consider a clear, hanging overdoor shoe bag to keep small cars, action figures, doll clothes, or art supplies easily visible.

Legos seem to be the bane of every parent's existence. There are many ways to store them, but the final decision will depend upon how the child plays with them. If he is a "sorter," then clear, plastic, lidded boxes sorted by color or size might be perfect. If he is a "dumper," then there is no sense sorting and a couple larger bins will do.

For toy storage in common areas — like living or family rooms — wicker baskets (lined or unlined with fabric) make attractive storage, and it's easy to drop toys into these no-lid containers at the end of each day. Rectangular-shaped baskets work well for kids' books because they can easily flip through the collection and find their favorites. Plastic bins on wheels make for easy transportation of toys from one room to another.

Organizing products from the kitchen can work wonders with art supplies. For example, a turntable keeps glue, glitter, markers, and paints at-the-ready.

Use a label maker or colorful markers on hanging tags to write the name of what's inside each container. This makes it easy for retrieval, and, even more importantly, for clean-up! For kids who can't yet read, glue photos or drawings of the objects on the front of the containers.

6. CLEAN UP & MAINTAIN

Put the donation box in the car or near the exit so it leaves the home immediately. Take out the trash. Grab the relocation box and redistribute all of its contents appropriately.

To maintain the toy area, help kids downsize every six months by donating seldom-used toys. Establish a "new toy in, old toy out" system where some purging takes place before shopping. Talk to them about how it feels — and how important it is — to donate to local charities.

setting toy limits

establish a "new toy in, old toy out" routine, especially before birthdays and the holiday gift-giving season

have the family research and then adopt a local charity that needs toys, and commit to donating there regularly

rotate toys every few months so they seem new again (send Barbie on a vacation in the attic or let some stuffed animals hibernate in the garage for the winter)

Organize a
LIVING SPACE

EXAMPLES OF STORAGE
- living room
- family room
- 3- or 4-season porch
- basement rec room

SUPPLIES NEEDED
- trash bags/recycling bin, donation box, relocation box, fix-it box
- spray cleaner and cleaning cloth
- broom and dust pan and/or vacuum
- functional furniture for storage
- storage containers
- label maker and/or tags to hang from containers/baskets

TIME COMMITMENT
- 3–9 hours

1. ASSESS & PLAN
Family living spaces (be it a living room, family room, or rec room) generally have a place for lounging (sofa, love seat, comfy chairs), tables (coffee table or ottoman, side tables, sofa table, desk), storage (bookshelves, cupboards, and/or entertainment center), and an electronics area (television, DVD player, stereo or MP3 dock, DVDs, CDs, gaming systems and games). Start by figuring out what types of activities take place in this space and if it functions well for them. Some living rooms need major decluttering, while others simply need better furniture arrangement and some easy out-of-sight storage solutions.

2. EMPTY, SORT & QUICK-TOSS
Check the quick-toss list to see what can be placed immediately into the trash/recycling bin. Then, gather categories of items together. For example, round up books from bookshelves, end tables, under the sofa, etc. (You might also gather up all books throughout the house if the goal is to consolidate and/or downsize all books.)

quick assessment questions

What activities take place here?
• • •
What would you ideally like this space to look like?
• • •
Does this space need to be decluttered or merely rearranged?

potential goals for this space

create a space that is multi-functional

create a cozy conversation area

hide visual clutter like DVDs and CDs

create hidden storage for toys

downsize book collection

create a space to pay bills or write letters

Other categories of living space items might include board and card games, books and magazines, DVDs and CDs, and video gaming items. If knick-knacks are an issue, gather them together. Wipe down the shelves as you go.

3. DECLUTTER
Once you can see your categories, consider the quantities, and begin to downsize. If decluttering is part of the plan, pick one area to start. For example, if books are overabundant, recognize the amount that will realistically fit within the bookshelves in this room, and then review and reduce them.

If electronic media needs some attention, tackle that area. (If you find old VHS tapes but no VHS player, this is a good time to let those go.) Board games can be released if they are never or seldom played. (Parents of high schoolers can probably get rid of the Candyland game!) If knick-knacks are taking over and making cleaning difficult, downsize the collection and then plan to display the rest in a lovely arrangement. Round up any papers that have made their way into the living room and place them all into a box to deal with later. (See the Paperwork section for detailed instructions.)

4. DECLARE A HOME
If you find anything that would be better off in another area of the home, place it into the relocation box for redistribution at the end of the project. This happens quite frequently in the living spaces!

Next, decide where categories of items will live. If the current storage areas work well, that is fine. But if storage is non-existent, insufficient, inconvenient, or unattractive, decide where the items should be moved to for maximum efficiency and ease-of-use. For example, many families with children get frustrated with toys littering their living rooms. Decide how many toys should be stored in this room, and brainstorm storage options to keep them corralled, yet easily accessible, such as in a wooden cubby or on a low bookshelf.

Now is also the time to do a little space planning. A living room needs to have good flow so people can easily pass through it. (At least 18 inches is needed for traffic lanes.) It also needs to be functional, so make sure that the television is easily viewed from the main seating area, if applicable. Make conversation time easy by arranging the sofa, loveseat,

quick-toss list

magazines more than two months old

any newspapers more than one day old

outdated catalogs

ripped or ratty throws/blankets

puzzles missing pieces

games missing pieces

old VHS tapes

old cassette tapes

moldy or damaged books

anything broken that isn't worth the effort to fix

and/or chairs in close proximity. Have a place to set a drink within arm's reach of each seat. If the family likes to work on puzzles, see if space can be carved out for a small table. In addition, find the room's focal point (such as a fireplace, television, grand piano, or stunning window view) and angle the furniture toward it.

5. CONTAIN & LABEL
It's important that living space storage is attractive and matches the decor of this space, especially if containers will be out in the open rather than hidden in a cupboard, armoire, or television storage unit. Rattan and wicker baskets can work with many living spaces, as can leather or fabric cubes. Don't forget to create a storage method for coffee table clutter, like remote controls. A wooden tray or open-top box often works well. Some things that may need to be contained include magazines, electronic gaming equipment, DVDs and CDs, board games/cards, and toys.

If the room has bookshelves, now is a good time to give them a little makeover. Hopefully, they have some breathing room on them after the decluttering phase. Intersperse books with family heirlooms, children's artwork, or a prized collection, and layer framed photos between and behind short stacks of books. Books can become a focal point in the room by running a stack horizontally instead of in the traditional vertical arrangement, and then topping it off with an eye-catching bowl or prized collectible. Or, use attractive boxes to corral clutter or categories of paperbacks on shelving for a less-busy feel.

6. CLEAN UP & MAINTAIN
Put the donation box in the car or near the exit so it leaves the home immediately. Take out the trash. Grab the relocation box and redistribute all of its contents appropriately.

Make a plan to tidy this living space daily, and to schedule an organizing maintenance session semi-annually.

storage containers

bins/boxes/baskets that are attractive enough to be displayed (fabric, wicker, leather, etc.)

bookends

cubby organizers, large or small

magazine file boxes

magazine rack

multimedia boxes

trays

Organize a KITCHEN

EXAMPLES OF STORAGE
- drawers
- cupboards
- pantry
- countertop/island

SUPPLIES NEEDED
- trash bags/recycling bin, donation box, relocation box, fix-it box
- spray cleaner and cleaning cloth
- broom and dust pan and/or vacuum
- storage containers
- label maker and/or tags to hang from containers/baskets

TIME COMMITMENT
- 6–12 hours

1. ASSESS & PLAN

Begin by analyzing the current storage systems. Are some things working well? If so, don't change them! If keeping a thermos on the counter by the coffee maker works, stick with it. If it's convenient to have recipe books on the countertop, keep it up. Now ponder anything inconvenient. How could you make those things work a little better? For example, if piles of cans and bottles litter the countertop as they await a trip outside for recycling, then make a new plan, such as clearing space under the sink to install a pull-out trash can to capture those recyclables immediately after use. If the morning cereal can't be found because it's stuffed in the overflowing pantry, then the pantry needs to be cleared out and reorganized.

If locating food is the first concern, then the pantry (or the food storage cupboards) is the place to start. If you'll also be reorganizing all the dishware, utensils, and storage containers, recognize that this project may take multiple days to complete.

quick assessment questions

What types of activities happen in this room besides meals?

• • •

What types of things need quick and instant access?

• • •

What categories of items can be downsized?

potential goals for this space

keep the kitchen table clear and ready for mealtimes

create a functional kitchen that makes meal prep easier

avoid over-buying

have countertops free of clutter

minimize messy paperwork on counters and table

2. EMPTY, SORT & QUICK-TOSS

Take everything out of the pantry or cupboards. Check the quick-toss list to see what can be placed immediately into the trash. As you go, separate items into categories like canned goods, pasta, rice, baking supplies, oils and vinegars, spices, breakfast foods, snacks, etc. You'll see categories develop. Sort into subcategories if applicable. (Canned goods could be broken down into vegetables, fruits, tomato products, soups, etc.) Or, if working on the dishware, utensils, and containers first, take those out and start sorting into categories like everyday dishes, special occasion dishes, baking dishes, cookie sheets, pots and pans, cutlery, storage containers, small appliances, etc. You'll also want to round up cleaning supplies.

If paperwork is taking over the kitchen, gather it all together in a large box, and plan to work on that at a separate time. See the Organize a Household Command Center section of this book for details.

3. DECLUTTER

Foods that are expired, of course, should be tossed. But if there is an overabundance of non-expired foods, consider donating them to a local food shelf. Make a note of excess items.

Did you unearth three dozen mismatched mugs? Are there any that can be tossed or donated? Is there a wide variety of plates, cups, and bowls? Pull sets together and select the favorite one. Can the others be donated or given to someone else? Assess pots and pans. Most people use two or three stockpots and two or three pans the majority of the time. Since pots and pans are quite bulky, encourage the donation of any not frequently used.

This is also a good time to inventory all small kitchen appliances. While purchased with good intentions, most (like the fondue pot or bread maker) are seldom or never used. Unless there is ample room to store these items, prioritize and keep only those things that are used on a regular basis.

quick-toss list

expired cans and boxes of foods

cans that are bulging

broken dishes

mugs received as freebies or souvenirs

plastic storage containers without lids

ratty dishcloths and towels

unused small appliances

unused cookbooks

florist vases

4. DECLARE A HOME

If you find anything that would be better off in another area of the home, place it into the relocation box for redistribution at the end of the project.

Keeping similar things together will help with easy kitchen navigation. For example, keep baking supplies together in one container so you can simply pull it out when it's time to bake. Store cleaning supplies under the sink in a caddy or two-tiered pull-out rack.

As you look over your groupings of kitchen items, plan to store them where they are used. For example, everyday dishes might work great directly above the dishwasher or close to the table. Perhaps pots and pans and cookie sheets could go near the stove. The coffee machine that is fired up daily should be easily accessible on the counter near the mugs, coffee beans, and grinder.

If something is used frequently, keep it close and convenient. Where we put our stuff is as important as what we own. If we can't find it when we need it, or it's inconvenient to reach, it's likely we won't use it!

Now is a good time to consider adding pull-out shelves on some lower-level cabinets. In addition, be sure to adjust cupboard and pantry shelving for efficient storage. This simple step takes only minutes to do, but many people forget or neglect to adjust shelving.

For things used infrequently, like the turkey roasting pan pulled out just twice a year, store them in the less-convenient storage spaces. Put them on the top shelf of a cupboard, in the hard-to-reach cupboard over the fridge, way in the back of a lower cupboard, or even stored in the basement, attic, or garage. (But be sure to keep all kitchen items together, in a clearly defined and labeled space, if moving them outside of the kitchen.)

If there is not enough storage space in a very tiny kitchen, consider adding a wire shelving unit or small, rolling island with storage underneath. And don't forget to use wall space.

5. CONTAIN & LABEL

Now that you can clearly see categories and all the keepers, decide on the type and size of containers you'll need. There are many helpful organizing products available to keep kitchens orderly. Baskets and bins come in a variety of sizes and hold foods, like onions and potatoes, as well as cleaning supplies. An attractive vase or crock near the stove top corrals cooking utensils. A hanging overdoor shoe bag on the back of the pantry door will neatly hold spice packets, Jello boxes, or kitchen gadgets.

To make a pantry more visually appealing, take single-serve snacks (like granola bars or fruit snacks) and pop them into an open-top bin. This makes it easier to locate and grab a snack, and reduces pantry clutter. Cereals can be dispensed into flip-top, easy-to-pour cereal canisters. Clear glass and plastic food storage boxes and canisters are widely available and provide neat and attractive storage for bulk items like lentils, rice, and pasta.

Many cooks struggle with how to organize their spices. An acrylic, wall-mounted spice rack or a set of tin containers combined with a magnetic spice rack mounted on the wall can save precious cupboard space. In-drawer spice racks make it easy to locate the cinnamon. Spice jars can be stored on a three-tiered expanding shelf. Basic glass spice jars can be separated into sweet and savory and stored in two shallow, open-top bamboo boxes in a cupboard. If there is enough counter space, you might opt for a spinning spice rack. Whatever method is chosen, don't store spices close to the stove or they'll lose their potency.

Double-decker wire stacking shelves, tiered cabinet risers, undershelf baskets, and Lazy Susan turntables will double storage space inside a cupboard. Pull-out cabinet organizers will make it easier to locate pots, pans, and lids on lower shelves. An undersink, two-tier sliding organizer will make cleaning supplies easily accessible. There are even products designed to make the inside of the fridge and freezer more tidy, such as soda can holders and a variety of plastic bins and baskets.

storage containers

bins/boxes/baskets that are open-top

bins/boxes/baskets with lids

bulk food storage containers

cabinet risers/ expanding shelves

cabinet shelves

cleaning caddies

drawer dividers

hanging overdoor shoe bags

lid organizers

stacking bins

stacking shelves

turntables

undershelf baskets

undersink pull-out baskets

undersink, two-tier sliding organizers

Label as much as possible so that it's easy to find what is needed. When putting away groceries or unloading the dishwasher, labels allow all family members to know the correct homes. To label a drawer, don't stick labels on the face of a drawer because it destroys the aesthetic appeal. Instead, put the label on the inside lip of the drawer so it is visible only when the drawer is opened. Likewise, inside a cupboard, label the front side of all shelves. Use a label maker to mark jars and canisters.

6. CLEAN UP & MAINTAIN

Put the donation box in the car or near the exit so it leaves the home immediately. Take out the trash. Grab the relocation box and redistribute all of its contents appropriately.

Make sure your have created an "in/out" system where some purging takes place before the purchase of a new item. If a new set of plastic storage containers is purchased, an equal amount of old Tupperware® should be donated. If a new mug comes home, an old one must go.

It may be helpful to stash a donation box somewhere nearby as an easy reminder of this rule. Also, set aside time twice a year to check expiration dates on canned and boxed foods, as well as to do a quick-purge of old items in the fridge and freezer.

Set aside time once each year to review the kitchen and all its contents. Discard anything broken, donate anything unused in the past 12 months, and determine if the storage systems still make sense for the entire household.

Organize a
GARAGE, ATTIC, OR BASEMENT

EXAMPLES OF STORAGE
- entire unfinished basement
- portion of basement
- garage
- attic

SUPPLIES NEEDED
- trash bags/recycling bin, donation box, relocation box, fix-it box
- spray cleaner and cleaning cloth
- broom and dust pan and/or vacuum/shop vac
- storage containers
- dumpster or "dumpster in a bag" (possibly)
- label maker and/or tags to hang from containers/baskets

TIME COMMITMENT
- 8–20 hours

1. ASSESS & PLAN

These storage spaces are likely a mixture of past, present, and future. Well-loved toys, grade school memorabilia, and furniture from the college years may make up memories from the past. Perhaps golf clubs, cold-weather clothing, and gardening tools reflect the present. Baby clothes or gear saved for a future child may represent the future.

Take note of the amount of "past" memories stored compared to the "current" and "future" items in the space. What goals and activities are on the to-do list in the upcoming months and years? Out with the old to make way for new hobbies and activities: a cleared-out attic could make a great artists' studio. A tidy basement might morph into a fabulous home theater. An organized garage could allow a budding woodworker or gardener room to grow.

quick assessment questions

What are the main categories of storage items?

• • •

Which categories could be greatly pared down?

• • •

What types of things need quick and instant access?

potential goals for this space

be able to fit the car(s) in the garage

be able to easily access sports or gardening equipment

store chemicals and paints away from children's reach

completely clear out the attic

get rid of childhood memorabilia to make room for new hobbies

2. EMPTY, SORT & QUICK-TOSS

Check the quick-toss list to see what can be placed immediately into the trash/recycling bin. (Be sure to set aside any chemicals so they can be taken to the local hazardous waste facility.)

The initial step to organizing a storage space — basement, attic, or garage — is to sort into categories. To begin the process, designate a sorting area — such as the driveway — or clear some floor space in a corner of the basement or attic. Then, item by item, start sorting into logical categories. Some might include automotive, crafting, clothing, home improvement, lawn and garden, memorabilia, sports equipment, seasonal items, tools, and toys. Each household is unique, so categories will mirror a family's lifestyle and priorities. Create categories based on how each family lives (or wants to live).

Next, create sub-categories. Clothing can be further divided by person, size, or season. Divide sports equipment by activity or season. You might break out tools into smaller everyday tools and larger power tools for special projects. One great thing about sorting is you'll easily see duplicate items so the next stage is easier.

3. DECLUTTER

Once you can see your categories, consider the quantities, and begin to downsize. (For extremely large purging jobs, consider renting a dumpster.)

Take a good look at the categories created and see if they reflect the family's current lifestyle and activities. Never going to play badminton again? Out go the rackets! Have the kids moved out of the house? Perhaps it's time to let go of their 20-year-old boxes of stuffed animals. If there is indecision about whether or not something should go, ask, "What's the worst thing that could happen if this is tossed?" Now is also the time to pare down duplicate items. Multiples of tools, an excess of lawn chairs, and boxes of Christmas decorations can be reduced to save space.

quick-toss list

dried up paints

chemicals no longer used or needed

sporting equipment in poor condition

old cardboard boxes being saved "just in case"

anything broken, stained, rusted, or mildewed

broken down or never used sports equipment, like treadmills or elliptical machines

outdated baby equipment

old cars that don't run and never will

bikes and helmets that don't fit anyone in the household

old newspapers or magazines

high school or college notebooks or textbooks

4. DECLARE A HOME

If you find anything that would be better off in another area of the home, place it into the relocation box for redistribution at the end of the project.

Now that items are sorted by category, decide on the best location for each group of items. Should they stay in their current space? You may determine that items once kept in the basement might be better off in the garage, or attic treasures should move to the basement, for example. Also think of storage areas in terms of zones: automotive, lawn and garden, sports, seasonal, tools/workbench, toys, etc. Here are some ideas for placement:

Basement: crafting, emergency supplies, out-of-season clothing, home improvement materials, durable (non-delicate) memorabilia, sports equipment, seasonal items, tools, toys

Attic: baby items saved for the next child or grandchildren, craft supplies, out-of-season clothing, furniture, luggage, durable (non-delicate) memorabilia, seasonal items, past tax documents

Garage: automotive, home improvement, lawn and garden, outdoor toys, seasonal items, sports equipment, tools

Things used frequently should be easily accessible. Place the heaviest items on the bottom, the most-used stuff at waist to eye level, and things that are rarely (or never) used high up or in the back. For example, special toys saved for future grandchildren can be placed in the attic or on a top shelf in the basement, while sports equipment needed daily or weekly can be stashed in the garage.

Note: When storing paints and chemicals, use caution. Paints need to be kept out of freezing temperatures, so garage storage is usually not a good idea. However, if you store them in the basement, be sure to keep them at least 10 feet from the hot-water heater and furnace so vapors aren't ignited by the gas flame. Consider a locked cabinet if there are young children in the home.

storage containers

boxes, clear plastic, with lids

hooks and brackets

lockable cabinet

pegboard

shelving

rolling or storage carts/chests

stackable bins

tall barrels

wall-mounted tool holders

In any storage space, make use of vertical space by investing in some sturdy shelving units. Your local hardware or home improvement store will have a wide selection. Shelving gets items up and off the floor, creating more space and a cleaner look. Some families like to purchase expensive custom storage systems, but something as simple as installing pegboard on one wall and hanging a few inexpensive hooks to hold bikes, rakes, brooms, sleds, ladders, and hoses can be helpful.

5. CONTAIN & LABEL

Consolidate items for easy retrieval, placing them as close as possible to where they will be used. For example, in the garage, keep gardening supplies in a large basket by the outside door. Set recycling bins right next to the interior door. Put tools on or near the workbench.

Once you decide on a location, put small- to medium-sized similar items in appropriately sized containers. For example, use labeled jars or a multi-drawer storage system to separate small pieces of hardware. Use lids on containers that don't need to be accessed frequently, or opt for no lids if the items are needed on a daily basis. Large 15–20 gallon plastic tote boxes with lids work well to store holiday decorations or anything that doesn't need to be accessed more than a couple times per year.

Sports equipment needed daily or weekly can be stashed in the garage in a tall can — hockey sticks, baseball bats, and other long items will be easy for kids to access and put away. Corral balls in a large bin.

Make sure the containers are well-labeled on the front and sides (not just the tops) for easy identification.

6. CLEAN UP & MAINTAIN

Put the donation box in the car or near the exit so it leaves the home immediately. Take out the trash. Grab the relocation box and redistribute all of its contents appropriately. If a dumpster was rented, call to have it retrieved.

Make a plan to maintain these spaces on a semi-annual basis so that the basement, attic, and garage don't become holding cells for clutter.

Organize a
CRAFT AREA

EXAMPLES OF STORAGE
- craft room
- craft closet
- armoire, hutch, desk, or cubbies

SUPPLIES NEEDED
- trash bags/recycling bin, donation box, relocation box
- spray cleaner and cleaning cloth
- broom and dust pan and/or vacuum
- storage containers
- label maker and/or tags to hang from containers/baskets

TIME COMMITMENT
- 3–9 hours

1. ASSESS & PLAN

Enthusiasm for crafting has hit an all-time high. Millions of people have taken on scrapbooking, card making, sewing, quilting, beading, and jewelry making as their new favorite pastimes. Figuring out where and how to store and organize all the accessories that go along with these hobbies can be a test in creativity and containerization. As you begin, determine if there is enough counter space on which to work. How about storage space? Does the hobby entail lots of little pieces (like beading) or does it require lots of flat storage for paper (like scrapbooking)? Since crafters are generally very visual, it can be helpful to look at photos of a variety of craft spaces, containers, and ideas. Check out Pinterest for craft storage inspiration.

2. EMPTY, SORT & QUICK-TOSS

As you begin emptying and sorting, check the quick-toss list to see what can be placed immediately into the trash can. Start sorting supplies into categories. For example, a gift-wrapping station might have wrapping paper, gift bags, ribbons, bows, tags, scissors, tape, and pens.

quick assessment questions

Which types of craft materials are stored in this space?

• • •

What needs to be kept close-at-hand?

• • •

What can be stored further away?

potential goals for this space

remove anything from the space not related to the hobby

declutter craft supplies

corral craft supplies in an eye-pleasing manner

make it easier to find craft supplies

neatly contain and clearly label craft supplies

keep craft supplies in good condition

3. DECLUTTER

Once you can see your categories, consider the quantities, and begin to downsize. Anything no longer needed or loved can be tossed or placed into the donation box. Crafters tend to accumulate a lot of new-fangled supplies and may not realize how much they have or that they have purchased similar or duplicate items. Sewers and quilters may have years' worth of fabric in boxes or bags, and once they see it all corralled in one spot, they may be able to get rid of those that are no longer fashionable or in good shape.

4. DECLARE A HOME

Since this space is dedicated to crafting, anything this is not related to the hobby should be placed into the relocation box for redistribution at the end of the project.

Now, a little space planning is in order. Since you have sorted and decluttered, everything that is left needs to fit in the space dedicated to crafting. If this space is an entire room, evaluate the layout. Is there enough counter/desk space to efficiently work on the craft? If not, where and how could you create more? Sometimes just adding a simple, foldable table makes a space more usable. Can shelving be added above the desk or table, or could you add a large cubbie-style unit on one wall for maximum storage opportunities?

Don't forget to use wall space. Pegboard isn't just for the garage. It can be added to a craft room to keep supplies at the ready. And since crafters are always on the lookout for new ideas, be sure to install a large bulletin board or magnet board for tacking up inspiration.

Since crafting usually involves lots of categories of supplies (and lots of small items that can get visually cluttered), consider closed-door cabinetry to keep the room looking tidy.

If there isn't an entire room dedicated to the craft, there are many other options, from an armoire or hutch to a rolling kitchen cart. Another idea is to add shelving in a laundry room or a closet. Just about any space can be turned into a small but efficient crafting space so long as it's organized.

quick-toss list

wrinkled or half-used craft papers

anything broken, rusty, moldy

sewing patterns that are the wrong size or out of fashion

fabric that is faded

scraps that are too small to be useful

dried-up adhesives

tools that are broken

5. CONTAIN & LABEL

Each hobby brings unique organizational challenges. Quilters and sewers will need storage for patterns and lots of fabric. Figure out a way to corral it (neatly folded) so that it is easy to see at a glance what is available for the next project. Beading and jewelry crafters will need very small, lidded containers to separate items.

Scrapbookers and cardmakers will need a way to sort and store a variety of decorative papers. Scrapbooking stores sell neat plastic storage boxes and paper sorters, but you can also look to office supply stores for letter trays, desktop file boxes, magazine file boxes, and even wall-mounted racks to hold these items. Three-ring binders filled with clear protector sheets can hold stickers, tags, or scraps of paper.

Don't overlook storage containers often reserved for other areas of the home. For example, spice tins can be used to store beads, buttons, pins, and grommets. Canning jars can be inexpensive, see-through storage for ribbon scraps, small stampers, or scrapbooking embellishments. Ribbon and spools of wire can be stored on a paper-towel holder. A tackle box or drawer dividers can help separate a jumble of needles, bobbins, and thimbles. Clear, over-the-door shoe organizers can create grab-and-go storage. And, of course, be sure to label every container you fill up.

Be sure to have separate containers for the multitude of markers, pens, pencils, scissors, and adhesives associated with scrapbooking and cardmaking. A turntable on the work surface can make them easy to access.

Don't forget that every type of craft has some papers associated with it, whether they are idea books, magazines, or ideas printed off the internet. Create a way to categorize and store them.

6. CLEAN UP & MAINTAIN

Put the donation box in the car or near the exit so it leaves the home immediately. Take out the trash. Grab the relocation box and redistribute all of its contents appropriately. Make a plan to sort through craft supplies once a year and toss or donate anything no longer needed.

storage containers

bins/boxes/baskets that are open-top

boxes, clear plastic, with lids in many sizes

bulletin boards

cubby organizers, large or small

document/office storage boxes

drawer dividers

peg board

letter trays

magazine file boxes

paper sorters

photo boxes

rolling or storage carts/chests

shelving

turntables

wall file/racks

Organize by
ECO-ORGANIZING

EXAMPLES
- reduce
- reuse
- recycle

SUPPLIES NEEDED
- non-toxic cleaning supplies
- eco-friendly organizing containers such as those made from bamboo or glass
- recycled organizing containers

TIME COMMITMENT
- 3–6 hours

1. ASSESS & PLAN
An eco-friendly organizing plan includes strategies to reduce, reuse, and recycle. This implementation will save the home-owners time and money; create an eco-friendly home; and protect the earth's resources. First, figure out what is being done in the "three R's" areas. Next, determine the area(s) that need some advice and guidance. For example, if the house-hold wants to recycle more, the solution may be to create a functional, aesthetically appealing recycling center in an accessible location. If the household has a lot of clutter, perhaps the goal is to downsize and donate the cast-offs to a favorite local charity. Whatever the reason for eco-organizing a home, start with a goal in mind to get the entire family on board.

2. EMPTY, SORT & QUICK-TOSS
This is the "reduce" phase. For any space that you are organizing, it will be easy to see duplicate and unnecessary items as you empty and sort the contents. Follow the quick-toss guide in the section of this book that corresponds with the space you are organizing. Be sure to dispose of any hazardous materials (like toxic cleaning products, household chemicals, or paints) according to local waste management guidelines. As you are quick-tossing, be sure to recycle as much as possible. As you are wiping down shelves, be sure to use non-toxic cleaning supplies.

quick assessment questions

Why do you want to organize your home in an eco-friendly manner?

• • •

What items are currently recycled in this household?

• • •

Would you like to buy less in the future?

potential goals for this space

find things easily so you can purchase less

use less energy

think of creative ways to reuse or reinvent old items in the organizing realm

locate appropriate charities to donate or recycle unneeded household items

set up a convenient recycling station in the home

3. DECLUTTER

Once sorted, it's easy to see duplicate and unnecessary items. Many people have issues with consumerism and over-abundance. To be more eco-conscious, you might recommend reducing overall shopping habits. Or, suggest that it's sometimes better to invest in a higher-quality, longer-lasting item that won't fall apart so quickly. You can also encourage the co-op of large purchases — such as snow blowers or lawn mowers— with neighbors, or simply borrow (like in the good old days) things that are needed only once in a while.

Now is also a good time to introduce a few ideas with regard to reducing consumption and energy use. For example, recommend turning off and unplugging electronics when not in use to avoid "vampire power usage;" use power strips to make shut-down easy; request a home energy audit; and purchase rechargeable batteries.

In the kitchen, homeowners can look for the Energy Star efficiency rating when replacing appliances, swap out standard incandescent light bulbs with CFLs to save energy and money, and use reusable cloth napkins instead of paper napkins. They can also keep reusable bags handy by the exit door or in the car to take along to stores.

In bathrooms, recommend buying shampoo/toiletries in bulk to reduce packaging, installing low-flow showerheads to reduce water consumption, using reusable rags/cloths for cleaning instead of paper towels, and purchasing or making only non-toxic cleaning products.

And don't overlook the importance of reducing the amount of junk mail entering the home. See the list in the sidebar for directions to get off mailing lists.

4. DECLARE A HOME

Another way to reduce consumption is to clear clutter and create easy-to-locate homes for things. When you know where to find things, you avoid making expensive, unnecessary, duplicate purchases.

reduce junk mail

get removed from direct marketing mailing lists by visiting www.dmachoice.org

opt out of paper catalogs you no longer enjoy by visiting www.catalog-choice.org

stop mailings of credit card and insurance offers by calling 1-888-5-OPT-OUT

opt out of receiving phone books by visiting www.dex-knows.com. Click "Select Your Dex" on the bottom and select "0" as the quantity of books you want to receive

5. CONTAIN & LABEL

Rather than purchasing new organizing containers, you might shop a thrift store like Goodwill or tag sales first. Used is more eco-friendly than new.

Another option is to reinvent common household items into the products you need to fit any space. There are many types of boxes that often get tossed in the trash or recycling bin that could be a perfect fit! For example, shoe boxes are the right size and shape for holding small gardening tools, sorting socks, or holding special cards. Tissue boxes can be used to store plastic shopping bags (when you need one, they pop out one at a time!) or to collect trash in the car. Check boxes can be configured into handy drawer dividers to organize office supplies, such as pens, rubber bands, index cards, note cards, and envelopes. Cardboard laundry detergent boxes and cereal boxes can be decorated with colored or patterned scrapbooking paper and used to hold magazines.

Jars and bottles also make great storage containers. Baby food jars help separate nails, screws, washers, and other hardware by size. Drum-shaped containers hold anything tall and lean, from kitchen implements to paintbrushes. Film canisters and mint tins hold tiny things like push pins or paper clips and make great travel buddies for jewelry. Just about any organizing product you need can probably be created by reusing common household containers.

If you can't find the organizing products you need used or from recycled household items, then shop smart. Look for containers with recycled content, and opt for glass, cotton, linen, bamboo, or cardboard over plastic. Before you shop, measure the space you need to fit so you buy exactly what's needed. If you can't find eco-friendly products in your local stores, consider shopping online. A good place to start is with the "eco-friendly" section at The Container Store.

homemade organizing containers

rectangular boxes, such as shoe boxes, laundry soap boxes, check boxes, mint tins, tissue boxes, cereal boxes

cylindrical-shaped containers, such as oatmeal cans, coffee cans, tall potato chip containers, film canisters, aluminum cans, gallon ice cream buckets

odd-shaped boxes, such as six-pack cardboard carriers, egg cartons

glass jars, such as baby food jars, mason jars

milk and juice cartons and jugs, laundry soap jugs

6. CLEAN UP & MAINTAIN

Put the donation box in the car or near the exit so it leaves the home immediately. Also, make smart decisions when it comes to recycling castoffs. Rather than discarding items in the trash, utilize your local donation resources. You may already know that you can donate clothing to Goodwill, but what about the extra lumber in the garage or old cell phones and eye glasses? Earth911.com is a good resource to find nearby charities that need unwanted items.

Then, make it easy for all family members to recycle. For example, in the family room or home office, place a small basket to toss in paper recycling. In the entryway and/or bedroom, keep a box stashed in the closet to capture items that need to go to the donation center. In the kitchen, make sure recycling bins are handy and easily accessible. You might even set up a small basket in the bathrooms for recycling empty shampoo and lotion bottles, cardboard packaging from toiletries (such as toothpaste and soap boxes) and even cardboard toilet paper tubes.

With just a few hours of hands-on work and eco-oriented organizing advice, it's easy to create a household that can follow the 3 R's, allowing households to reach their goals of living in an eco-friendly home.

Organize
TIME & SCHEDULES

SUPPLIES NEEDED
- large family wall calendar or online calendar system, like Cozi, Google Calendar, or iCal
- task management system, like a notebook, or online list-making tool such as Evernote

TIME COMMITMENT
- 2–4 hours

1. ASSESS & PLAN

While time doesn't take up physical space in a home, a family's schedule can be filled with extraneous clutter, confusion, and disharmony. Create a plan to organize a household's time, schedules, and tasks by following the same six-step process discussed throughout this book.

First, determine the current barriers to getting schedules under control. Are family members forgetting about important events? Are they always running late? Are there too many activities, leading to stress and frustration? Do they need a way to communicate important dates to one another? Figure out what needs to be fixed, and then create a plan to do it. Then look at household tasks. Are they equally distributed? Are there any that just aren't getting done?

2. EMPTY, SORT & QUICK-TOSS

Take a look at the current calendar, reviewing last month's, this month's, and next month's activities. Grab a notebook and jot down categories of appointments, such as sports activities, kids' extracurriculars, parties, worship events, after-hours work events, medical appointments, and any other family obligations that occur regularly. Do not include regular school and work hours. Those are a given and usually cannot be changed. Add up the time spent on each activity per week and month.

quick assessment questions

Are you frequently running late? Why?

• • •

If you had more time, how would you spend it?

• • •

Where are you wasting time?

potential goals

identify activities that are taking too much time

identify tasks that never seem to get done

find time for family members to eat meals or spend quality time together

dedicate time for exercise or relaxation

ensure all family members know the current schedule

arrive on time for all appointments and activities

Also, estimate how much time is spent on household chores and other tasks (like running errands or fixing things around the house). On a piece of paper, make a column for each family member, and then jot down each chore/task that he/she is responsible for and how much time is needed for each per week.

3. DECLUTTER

Take a look at time spent on each category of activity and task. Is there anything that is obviously monopolizing time? Are kids' sports activities forcing parents to divide and conquer every night of the week? Are there too many birthday parties or after-work events? Are there at least a few nights a week where everyone eats a meal or spends time together as a family? Figure out if too much time is being spent on any person or activity. If so, discuss reducing it in the future.

4. DECLARE A HOME

While many people use their smartphones or an online or computer-based calendar, every household still needs an all-inclusive wall calendar. It should list all activities for everyone in the family, excluding standard work and school hours. (Exception: If a person's work schedule is ever-changing, the hours will need to be noted on the calendar each day.) There are a variety of wall calendars available at office supply stores and online. Make sure to get one with lots of space to write appointments. (A great option is the Big Grid Family Wall Calendar, available on Amazon.) There are also the write-on/wipe-off whiteboard varieties, which work well if schedules change often. The downside to those, however, is that each month is wiped away every four weeks, so there is no way to look back on prior months' schedules should the need arise.

If the family prefers to use an online calendar, like Google calendar, Cozi, or iCal, that will work fine. The beauty of these is that individual family members can access the calendar from work or school and make changes on the fly from their computer or smartphone. It's so convenient! However, the calendar still needs to be printed out and posted in the Household Command Center for easy viewing. Take note that if frequent schedule changes are added online, an updated calendar will need to be printed out weekly, and quite possibly daily.

task tips

be realistic about how long each task will take

for little things that take only a minute or two (such as putting away dirty dishes or signing a permission slip), sometimes it's best to do them right away

if a task will take 15 minutes or more, choose a specific time to do it

break down large tasks into smaller chunks

work with daily rhythms and habits, such as being an early bird or night owl

delegate some tasks so you can free yourself to focus on where you can make your best contribution

learn to say "no" sometimes

As far as tasks go, it's time to set up a system. Notes scribbled on sticky notes and the backs of napkins do not count as a task management system. Use either a notebook or an online program or application like Evernote or Google Tasks to jot down tasks. This will include shopping lists and errands that need to be completed.

It also includes any household projects in the works. Make a list of all current projects. Which ones have been outstanding the longest? Are they still really essential? If the answer is, "not really," then take them off the list. It also will be helpful to break down large tasks into manageable chunks. For example, if a task is to plan a birthday party, then jot down "order cake, send invitations, buy decorations, clean house, pick up cake, food, and balloons." That way, it's easy to see what needs to be done, and possibly delegate parts of the list to family members. Schedule time on the calendar to complete larger tasks as needed.

5. CONTAIN & LABEL

With regard to the family calendar, some households like to use colored markers to designate activities for specific family members. Others prefer to use pencil so that activities can be deleted or changed without messing up the calendar. There is no "right" way to do it. Sometimes, trial and error is the only way to figure out what works best. Many online and computer-based calendars allow easy color customization.

6. CLEAN UP & MAINTAIN

The family should hold a short meeting each Sunday evening to review the upcoming week's activities. Everyone, even kids, should know how to use the calendar.

The family should use the task management system faithfully instead of relying on scraps of paper to remember what to do. With to-do lists that are ever-growing, writing down tasks and assigning the larger ones to a calendar can be a simple way to manage time and reduce stress. The simple act of writing down the things we need to do releases us from having to remember it all "upstairs."

time tips

figure out the real time it takes to accomplish a variety of routine responsibilities by using a kitchen timer to measure time

most unpleasant tasks don't take as long as you think they will

most pleasant things tend to drag out a bit longer than you'd expect

don't double-book or plan appointments too close together

plan for delays to keep calm

forget about multitasking once in a while

organizing paperwork & photos

It's often difficult to get
a handle on a home's
overwhelming piles of papers.
This section will teach you
how to organize a
home office and its
mountain of paperwork.
In addition, you'll learn how
to set up a household
command center, followed by
a photo organizing primer.

Organize a
HOME OFFICE

EXAMPLES OF STORAGE
- desk
- filing cabinet
- shelving/cubbies
- closet

SUPPLIES NEEDED
- trash bags/recycling bin, donation box, relocation box, fix-it box
- spray cleaner and cleaning cloth
- broom and dust pan and/or vacuum
- storage containers
- label maker and/or tags to hang from containers/baskets

TIME COMMITMENT
- 4–8 hours (doesn't include organizing paperwork)

1. ASSESS & PLAN

First, determine how the office space is used. (Please note, this section is addressing a home office that takes up a dedicated room. For info on how to set up a smaller paper management center that can be located within other rooms of the house, please reference the Organize a Household Command Center section of this book.)

You'll need to know what types of activities take place in the office. What tasks take place in this space? Some ideas might include bill paying, filing papers, working on the computer, talking on the phone, writing letters or working on writing projects, doing creative projects like drawing or painting, or reading. Some people actually use a home office for their work (whether they have a home-based business or they work from home on a regular basis), so figure out the tasks done daily. If the space is being used only for home tasks, who has access to the space and how is it used daily?

quick assessment questions

What is the purpose of this room?

• • •

What kinds of things should not be in this room?

• • •

Will all papers reside in this space, or will some go in the kitchen "Household Command Center?"

potential goals for this space

clear off all desk surfaces

set up a new, improved filing system

purge old filing cabinet's contents

go paperless by scanning papers

make bill paying easier

Then, figure out what is not working in that space. Not enough storage options? Maybe adding shelving or cubbies would help. Is the room a dumping grounds for non-office items? Perhaps you need to set guidelines for the types of items that will live in this space. Is paperwork causing issues? Figure out what types of papers frequently enter the room.

Please note that this section recommends gathering all papers together and handling them as a second stage to the home office organization project. Focus on non-paperwork items first for maximum impact and efficiency.

2. EMPTY, SORT & QUICK-TOSS

It will be helpful to start on the desktop with the most recently received items. Begin removing and sorting items. Gather all papers from the desktop and place them in one large box labeled "desktop papers."

Gather any papers on the floor or under the desk and place them in a second box labeled "floor papers." (These are likely older, less-needed papers.) Set aside paperwork for round two of this project. (See the Paperwork section of this book for instructions.) You may be moving inactive files to storage later, but for now, just keep all the papers together.

A quick note about the "paperless" office — it doesn't exist, and probably never will. There are some documents that need to be kept in hard-copy format, including tax documents, legal documents, and the like. That being said, there are ways to make a home or office have less paper. First, switch to online bill paying whenever possible, and opt to receive banking and financial statements via email. Second, consider the purchase of a personal scanner to store documents as PDFs on a computer. Scanners are available at a variety of price points. A couple goods ones are the Fujitsu ScanSnap and NeatDesk. There are also scanners that are made specifically for scanning receipts, such as NeatReceipts. There are even smartphone apps — like Lemon — that allow users to scan, digitize, and file receipts with their phones.

quick-toss list

manuals for items
no longer owned

outdated software
installation CDs

outdated or broken
office equipment

pens that don't work

stubby pencils

scraps of paper

unimportant receipts

unidentifiable keys

dead batteries

Once the papers are out of the way, put all office supplies into one pile, and then further sort those by type. What other categories of things show up in this space? You'll likely find some that really don't belong in an office space. Once a drawer, shelf, or desktop is clean, wipe it down.

3. DECLUTTER

Check the quick-toss list to see what can be placed immediately into the trash/recycling bin. Once you can see the categories, consider the quantities and begin to downsize. Get rid of outdated materials and equipment. Reduce office supplies down to an amount that will truly be used. Toss (or recycle) paper that is in no condition to go through a printer.

4. DECLARE A HOME

If you find anything that would be better off in another area of the home, place it into the relocation box for redistribution at the end of the project.

Based on the activities that take place here (as identified in step one), you'll want to place items needed for specific tasks near their point of use. For example, daily-use office supplies might go on the desktop or in the top desk drawer, while paper might be located near the printer.

Now is also the time to do a little space planning. Is the desk in an optimal place for getting work done? Is the lighting sufficient? Would it be helpful to add bookshelves, cubbies, floating shelves, or another type of wall storage? If there is a closet in the room, should shelves be added or adjusted? Is there sufficient filing cabinet space? (A good filing system starts with a great filing cabinet. Find one that opens easily and has plenty of usable space.) Is the chair comfortable? Should you add a small table in addition to the desk for creative writing or meetings?

5. CONTAIN & LABEL

Try to think vertically, rather than just horizontally. Use wall space to mount a bulletin board to hang a to-do list, frequently called phone numbers, and inspirational ideas. Install pegboard or a wire grid on the wall to hang supplies up and off the desk. Install shelving over the desk to hold books and reference materials. Mount the computer monitor on a swing arm from the wall. Visit a local office supply store

storage containers

bins/boxes/baskets that are open-top and with lids

bookends

bulletin boards

clipboards

desktop step file, file sorter, or file box

document/office storage boxes

drawer dividers

hanging overdoor shoe bags

letter trays

magazine file boxes

paper sorters

photo boxes

rolling or storage carts/chests

shelving, floating shelves

stackable bins

wall file/rack

for hanging organizing equipment, such as wall-mounted file pockets, to keep important files in plain view.

Then look beneath for hidden space. Fill a rolling storage cart (they come in a variety of drawer sizes) with supplies or promotional literature. Then roll it away under the desk or table. Don't forget to use the space behind the door — hang a shoe bag, and fill it with office supplies.

There are many helpful organizing tools and containers for office organization. Drawer dividers are essential to corral pens, paper clips, rubber bands, note pads, and more. Photo boxes, stackable bins, or any type of lidded boxes can corral office supplies by category.

Paper management is made easy with inexpensive organizing products. For example, a step file rack is great for keeping current projects on display, yet neatly in folders. Magazine holders are helpful for grouping reference materials such as catalogs, trade magazines, and newsletters. Clipboards come in a variety of colors and sizes, and they hold everything from current projects to reading material and can be taken on the road. Lidded cardboard storage boxes will be helpful if the filing cabinets are running out of room, so you can box up inactive files and store them off-site (once you've already purged all you can).

6. CLEAN UP & MAINTAIN

Put the donation box in the car or near the exit so it leaves the home immediately. Take out the trash. Grab the relocation box and redistribute all of its contents appropriately.

Make a plan to maintain this space on a quarterly basis.

(Note: For round two of an office organizing project, see the next section, Organize Paperwork, to tackle the boxes of paperwork you set aside.)

Organize
PAPERWORK

EXAMPLES OF STORAGE
- standard or lateral filing cabinet
- desktop filing box
- desk drawer with file rails installed
- cardboard bankers/storage boxes
- three-ring binders
- magazine/literature boxes
- document boxes

SUPPLIES NEEDED
- trash bags/recycling bin, relocation box
- spray cleaner and cleaning cloth
- broom and dust pan and/or vacuum
- file folders, hanging file folders, labels, shredder
- storage containers
- label maker and/or tags to hang from containers/baskets

TIME COMMITMENT
- 6–20 hours

1. ASSESS & PLAN

Organizing paperwork is a time-intensive project that requires a lot of focus. There will be times of frustration and boredom during some paperwork organizing projects, so it will be helpful to keep the goals in mind. Be sure to clarify why organizing the space is a priority.

As the project begins, there are many questions to ask, including what type of filing systems are currently being used (if any)?; what papers need to be kept easily accessible?; what types of papers need to be kept for archival or historical purposes?; as papers are received, what needs to be done with them, such as act, file, delegate, or toss?; how can to-do's be handled?; and who else in the home/office needs access to the papers?

The following basic system works well for most paper organizing projects. Of course, each household's needs are unique, and there are dozens (if not hundreds) of paper organizing techniques out there. Whether you use a simple file folder

quick assessment questions

What types of papers do you reference frequently?

• • •

What types of papers do you not want to receive anymore?

• • •

How do you currently process mail and other papers?

potential goals for this space

create a pleasant atmosphere in which to work or live

make it easy to locate important paperwork

eliminate paper piles

reduce the amount of papers entering this space

understand how to process paperwork

scan/go paperless

plus labels system or you opt to purchase an out-of-the-box paperwork organizing system (like Paper Tiger or Freedom Filer), you'll use the same process of sorting, decluttering, declaring a home, containing, and labeling.

2. EMPTY, SORT & QUICK-TOSS

Start on desktops, countertops, or urgently needed surfaces. The most recently received papers will be here, so round them up and place them all in a large box labeled "desktop papers."

Then, gather any papers that are on the floor or that are stuffed into paper bags, boxes in closets, or under desks and place them in a second box labeled "floor papers." (Resist the urge to start with these. They are likely older, less-needed papers.) It is important to round up all paperwork throughout the entire home if you are focusing on a home-based (rather than office) organizing job. Papers have a way of migrating throughout a home, and you'll need to see all categories of paperwork that are received on a regular basis.

Check the quick-toss list to see what can be placed immediately into the trash. As a surface becomes clear, wipe down the shelves and/or sweep or vacuum the floor so it's a clean slate.

Once all the papers are rounded up, determine the types of papers received on a regular basis as you start sorting. Pick up the top piece of paper from the "desktop papers" box. Ask, "What is this? Do you need to keep it? Do you need to take action on this? Or do you just need to file it in case you need to retrieve it later?" Make piles, using large sticky notes to label the piles, or pop them into temporary file folders as you sort. Remember that we generally use only about 20 percent of what we have, so keep the goal in mind to toss as much as possible.

As you encounter papers that need to result in an action, put them in a folder labeled "to do" (such as a class to sign up for, an RSVP to send, etc.). Be sure to enter upcoming events immediately on calendars and then toss the paper invitation. As you encounter invoices/bills that need to be paid, put them into a folder labeled "to pay." As you encounter papers that need to be discussed with significant others or coworkers, put them into a folder labeled "to discuss." As you encounter papers that simply need to be read and

quick-toss list

junk mail, such as catalogs, ads, and promotional mailers

newspapers older than one day

magazines older than two months, unless the plan is to keep a collection of a frequently referenced publication

anything expired: coupons, warranties, policies, invitations

manuals for items no longer owned

rough sort categories

to do

to pay (bills)

to discuss

to read

to file: active

to file: reference

then disposed of (magazine article clippings, newsletters, etc.), put them into a folder or basket labeled "to read." This is handy to take along when waiting in lines (such as at the doctor's office, dentist, bank, mechanic). Or the basket can be stored in the bathroom (really, a great place to read!), or near a favorite reading chair.

3. DECLUTTER

At this point, the remainder of the papers should be either thrown out/recycled, shredded, or filed into "active" or "reference" categories. Active files will likely go into a desktop file box kept either on the desktop or in the Household Command Center. (See next section for details.) Reference files will likely be stored in a filing cabinet in a home office. A recommended category list for the active filing grouping can be found in the sidebar. A category listing for the reference grouping is found in the appendix. Remember, "active" papers are those that need to be accessed on a daily or weekly basis. "Reference" papers need to be kept, but are rarely accessed.

Use colored folders if that seems helpful. (Color jogs memory for some, but not for others. For example, green might represent financial info or red for health papers.) Straight-line filing (where the top file tabs are all on the left, middle, or right instead of alternating file tab positions) creates a clean line that's visually appealing and easy to scan. Label folders and hanging-file tabs clearly, using a label maker or neat handwriting.

Work on clearing all surfaces of paper using the above techniques. Then, conquer the remaining piles (if any) from the floor or elsewhere. You should find there is more in the "toss" category in these piles. Remember, only 20 percent of the things we file will ever be retrieved again. Another option for reference papers is to scan them and then toss them, creating a paperless filing system on the computer.

4. DECLARE A HOME

If you find anything that would be better off in another area of the home, place it into the relocation box for redistribution at the end of the project.

Every household or office needs an appropriate type of file cabinet or box; the size will depend on the amount of papers

active filing categories

to pay (bills)

to do: high priority

to do: lower priority

to discuss

to read

. . . .

extracurriculars

home projects in process

medical/health

pending/waiting

receipts

school (per person)

work (per person)

(note: each household is unique, so create active file folders for anything in the family's life that is a daily or weekly occurrence)

reference filing categories

these can be found in the appendix

one must keep. Once the papers are downsized and sorted, you'll have a good idea of the type and size of filing storage system needed. Many households function well with a filing cabinet located in a home office or out-of-the-way space for papers that need to be kept simply for reference. (Think tax returns or product manuals.) But there also needs to be a convenient place to store the "active," daily or weekly-used papers. For many, this is a filing drawer or a desktop file box kept in the home's hub of activity, such as the kitchen. This box becomes part of a Household Command Center described in the next section.

5. CONTAIN & LABEL

Once you've determined where the paperwork will live, contain it in whatever storage container makes sense for the amount of papers. The file folders created can be stored in a file cabinet, desktop sorter, or whatever combination of containers make sense for the household. Just don't cram too much into a cabinet or it will be difficult and frustrating to retrieve and refile.

6. CLEAN UP & MAINTAIN

Take out the trash/recycling. Grab the relocation box and redistribute all of its contents appropriately.

Paper must be managed daily. Mail should be sorted as received, and junk mail should be tossed immediately. Everything else should be sorted into the active or reference-only filing systems. Homeowners should make time daily or weekly to file and can ask, "How am I going to use this?" Is it for a current project? File it in the appropriate folder in your active/desktop filebox. Is it historical or for future reference? File it in the filing cabinet. Is it something that needs action, such as a class to research? Put it in the "to do" file. Is it something to be read? Put it in the "to read" folder or basket. Is it something that needs to be discussed with a spouse or coworker? Put it in the "to discuss" folder. Ideas to minimize paperwork include removing and replacing documents on an annual basis, such as insurance statements. Each time a file is opened to retrieve something, include a 30-second review to see what can be tossed.

Make a plan to maintain this space on a semi-annual basis.

Organize a
HOUSEHOLD COMMAND CENTER

EXAMPLES OF STORAGE
- space in kitchen
- writing desk in living room
- hutch in dining room
- storage drawer on wheels

SUPPLIES NEEDED
- trash bags/recycling bin, donation box, relocation box
- spray cleaner and cleaning cloth
- broom and dust pan and/or vacuum
- file folders, hanging file folders, labels
- shredder
- desktop file box, file drawer, or step file for "active" categories of papers
- 3-ring binder to create a household reference binder
- cubby boxes/cubes, file folders, letter trays, or slots in a hanging document sorter, to serve as a "mail room"
- family calendar
- white board, chalk board and/or cork board for messages
- storage containers like magazine or document storage boxes
- label maker and/or tags to hang from containers/baskets

TIME COMMITMENT
- 3-6 hours (more time if all household paperwork needs to be organized)

1. ASSESS & PLAN
A Household Command Center includes a centrally-located, easily accessible filing drawer or desktop filing box for papers that are needed on a daily or weekly basis. In addition to a filing system, the command center is a place to process daily incoming mail and other papers; a place to keep and maintain a family calendar; a place to keep a handy contact list; and a place for family messages and communications.

potential goals for this space

make it easy to find frequently used phone numbers

create a system to get messages between family members

make it easy to find important papers

get a handle on the mail and school papers entering the home

have a place for take-out menus

Begin by figuring out where paper comes from, such as in the mail box, home with the kids from school, printed emails, handouts from work or conferences, receipts from store purchases, and sticky note communications from work colleagues or family members. Brainstorm a couple of location options for the new command center.

2. EMPTY, SORT & QUICK-TOSS

Setting up a Household Command Center involves creating a paper management system, so you'll likely be handling a backlog of paperwork. You'll need to create a filebox of "active" papers that have *daily relevance* to the household.

Start by gathering all recently received papers (usually those on counters and tables) into one big pile or box. (As you go, check the quick-toss list to see what can be placed immediately into the trash/recycling bin/shredder.) Now, sort the remaining papers into categories that make sense to the household, such as any of these:

- School: Have one folder per child
- Work: Have one folder per adult
- To Do: Have one folder per adult
- Bills to Pay: Keep these separate from other mail
- Pending/Waiting/Orders: Stash order confirmations here
- To File: Holds non-active papers that need to be filed later in a "reference" filing cabinet elsewhere
- Extracurricular Activities: Sign-up sheets, info, rosters, etc.
- Receipts: For those who want to keep them until credit card statements arrive
- Church/Worship: Holds schedules, class information, etc.
- Medical/Health and Fitness: Current papers that need to be referenced frequently, not all past medical history
- Home Improvement: If currently remodeling or involved in a large project

Try to limit it to 12–15 file folders. Write out the paper tabs with the category names. Use felt-tip pens, Sharpies, or a label maker for easy readability. Insert the tabs into the hanging file folders and keep the folders in the file box.

If you find papers that might need to be kept for reference/archive, but do not have *daily relevance* to the household, set those aside in a pile to file elsewhere, such as a filing

quick-toss list

junk mail, such as credit card offers and catalogs

expired coupons

newspapers older than one day, magazines older than two months

school papers that are unimportant (such as run-of-the-mill graded homework assignments)

shred-it list

"checks" that come with credit card statements

credit card offers for new accounts

credit card statements

paycheck stubs

receipts from ATM and debit card transactions

receipts from credit card purchases

returned checks

utility bills

cabinet in the home office or basement. These will be "reference-only" files. (See Paperwork section for details.)

3. DECLUTTER

Once sorted into categories, you'll likely see redundancies and an overabundance of certain categories of papers. Be sure to keep just the most recent versions of papers, and be ruthless with kids' school papers.

This is a good time to discuss the types of papers that should be saved or tossed. Each household will have its own preferences. For example, some want to keep monthly utility bill statements and quarterly investment statements for reference, while others prefer to toss them as soon as they are paid and/or reviewed.

Check the shred-it list, and contact a local shredding company if there is more paper than a personal shredder can handle. They'll come to a home or office, load up the papers to be shredded, and often times shred them right then and there with industrial-sized shredding machines. Or, they'll place the paper in a locked container and take it to their facility to shred.

4. DECLARE A HOME

If you find anything that would be better off in another area of the home, place it into the relocation box for redistribution at the end of the project.

Decide where you will locate the family command center. It is helpful to put it near where people are entering and exiting the home and where the family spends a lot of time, so often the kitchen works well for many families. The command center set-up could be on the counter, in a cupboard, or on a small table. It also could be located in a dining room, living room, or any space that is the hub of that household. It could even be mobile by utilizing a rolling cart.

Vital documents should be stored in a secure location like a fire-proof safe (locked and hidden) or off-site in a safe-deposit box.

vital documents

birth/death/adoption/citizenship certificates

investment/financial certificates

life insurance papers

long-term contracts

marriage/divorce documents

military records

passports

real-estate transaction documents

tax return documents

wills/estate papers

5. CONTAIN & LABEL
In addition to the filing system, a Household Command Center has a few other essential elements:

- a household reference binder
- a mail station
- a large wall calendar
- a bulletin board or magnetic board to post frequently called phone numbers, lunch menus, etc.
- a white board or chalk board to jot messages to one another (not to be used for doodling, and be sure to erase messages as soon as possible to avoid a messy, cluttered board)
- a drawer or container to hold everyday office supplies
- a nearby phone, as well as a trash/paper recycling bin and a small paper shredder

HOUSEHOLD REFERENCE BINDER
In addition to the filing box, some families may also benefit from a "household reference binder." It contains papers that the family wants to have at its fingertips, such as restaurant menus and phone number lists. It is an easy grab and go option, and can be a nice complement to a desktop file box. Some category ideas are listed in the sidebar. All that's needed to set one up is a 3-ring binder, tabbed dividers, and some 3-ring clear sheet protectors or 3-hole binder pockets. Write the category names on the tabs. Stash papers within the sheet protectors or binder pockets. Keep the binder located in the Household Command Center.

THE MAIL STATION
A mail station is a method to sort and distribute papers (daily mail, permission slips to sign) to each household member. Set up cubby boxes/cubes, file folders, "in box" letter trays, slots in a hanging document sorter, or whatever method you can dream up to create a "mail box" for each member of the household.

Locate this within the Household Command Center. Make sure the mail boxes are clearly labeled. Family members need to be trained to immediately put papers into the mail box of the intended recipient. When kids get home from school, they should unload back packs and place anything for mom or dad into the appropriate mail boxes. Have each

reference binder categories

day care/babysitting

gift-giving/birthdays/party planning

meal planning/grocery list templates

errands/shopping lists

restaurant menus and coupons

phone numbers/directories

school/lunch menus

sports/extra-curricular/team rosters

vacation/travel/fun activities

person check his/her mail box each day and completely clear it out and process papers as needed. These are not to be holding bins for papers or junk!

FAMILY CALENDAR
Busy families need a household calendar. By having one central location to jot down activities, meetings, and appointments, the entire family will function more smoothly. Some things to include are: vacation days from work and school, medical appointments, after-school activities, sports practices and games, trips, parties, play dates, and meetings.

There are a variety of sizes and layouts of wall calendars at the local office supply store or online. Online tools, such as Cozi or Google Calendar, offer a web-accessible calendar. If this option is used, the family will need to print out an updated version each week and find a convenient place to hang it, such as in the kitchen.

Instruct all family members to add their activities to the calendar as often as possible. Have everyone (including kids) look at the calendar each morning so they are aware of the day's activities. Hold a brief family meeting each Sunday evening to go over the upcoming week's events.

While family members may still have their own individual calendars, planners, or smartphone scheduling systems, remind them of the importance of communicating schedules to all family members through the family calendar.

6. CLEAN UP & MAINTAIN
Take out the trash/recycling. Grab the relocation box and redistribute all of its contents appropriately.

Create a plan to deal with incoming papers on a daily basis. Reduce the number or frequency of newspaper or magazine subscriptions. Receive and pay bills online to eliminate paper clutter. Request to receive financial statements online only. Keep mailing addresses private.

The file box and binder should be weeded out quarterly.

storing school papers

banker's boxes or file boxes holding one file folder per child, per grade

3-ring binder filled with clear protector sheets, divided by grade

artist's portfolio to hold oversized artwork

underbed storage box to hold artwork, one per child

take photos of 3-dimensional or oversized artwork to place in photo album or scrapbook

Organize
PHOTOS

EXAMPLES OF STORAGE
- photo albums/binder with photo sheets
- photo storage boxes
- accordion file box
- heavy-duty plastic (poly) envelopes
- digital storage: on computer, external hard drive, flash drive, and/or backed up on website

SUPPLIES NEEDED
- trash bags/recycling bin, share box
- sorting method, such as large envelopes or sorting box
- preferred storage method(s)
- label maker

TIME COMMITMENT
- depends upon quantity of photos

1. ASSESS & PLAN
Recognize that organizing a photo collection will take some time — especially if there are decades' worth of photos to organize — but with regular maintenance, the collection will offer a lifetime of enjoyment.

Before you begin, recognize the reason for starting this process. Perhaps it's to preserve and share memories. Or maybe it's just to eliminate those scattered piles of photos and negatives once and for all. Whatever the reasons, keep them in mind throughout the organization process.

2. EMPTY, SORT & QUICK-TOSS
The first step to creating an organized collection is to gather the photos all in one place. In addition to any photo albums, check everywhere for hidden photos — attics, basements, files, closets, under the beds. Decide on a large, central work surface, such as the dining room table or an out-of-the-way floor. Find a space that will be undisturbed so you won't feel rushed to finish.

quick assessment questions

What does the end result look like? Photo albums, boxes, digital?

• • •

Do you prefer to sort chronologically, or by event, person, or family?

• • •

Who might enjoy receiving extra or duplicate photos?

potential goals for this space

create archival-quality storage

share photo collection with other family members

gather all photos into one space

go digital with some or all photos

create electronic back-up of important photos

Now, sort the photos. This is the part that will take the longest, but it goes quickly once a system is in place. The most common way to sort is chronologically. This works well as most people's minds think chronologically. As photos are sorted, place them into labeled stacks, envelopes, or boxes by year. (Or use a handy box sorter made especially for this purpose.) Once sorted by year, go one step further and sort again by month, if you desire. If narrowing down to a specific year is difficult, just sort the photos into decades. If the sorting process feels overwhelming, start with the most recent ones first and save the older ones for later.

Another way to sort is by broad category or theme. For example, sort by events such as vacations, holidays, or weddings, or by family members or sides of the family. Create a mystery photo box for later research at family reunions for photos that need family input. Just like any organizing project, it's important to group similar objects together to see what and how much has accumulated.

3. DECLUTTER
Check the quick-toss list to see what can be placed immediately into the trash. Once the sorting process is complete, check for duplicates that can be tossed or shared with someone else. If you find 25 photos of little Johnny's third birthday party, perhaps some can be shared with the grandparents. Or consider enlarging and framing some favorites. And remember, it's okay to toss any photos that simply aren't liked.

4. DECLARE A HOME
Plan to store the photos away from light, heat, and humidity. Attics, basements, and garages are prone to extreme heat fluctuations, moisture/humidity, rodents, and insects. There-fore, they may not be the proper places for your most prized possessions. Protect photos so they last a lifetime. Watch for rodents and insects, and deal with them promptly to avoid damage.

quick-toss list

blurry photos

overexposed or dark photos

duplicate photos

photos that are out of focus

photos that are off-center

photos containing people you can't identify

stuck-together photos

Here are a few thoughts about scanning and digital storage. If there is a small amount of photos to be scanned (say, under 100), that is easy enough to tackle at home with a flatbed scanner or a portable scanner like the Fujitsu ScanSnap. Make sure to scan at 300–600 dpi for print-quality photos. Consider a scanning service for a larger quantity of photos. Simply mail them the photos and in just a couple weeks, they'll be sent back along with a DVD containing all the scans.

If photos are stored digitally on a computer, be sure to create folders and subfolders on the hard drive rather than dumping them all into one large photo collection. Use the same categories used with printed photos, such as sorting by year or event. Most importantly, digital storage requires at least one back-up system, such as on DVDs, flash drives, or an external hard drive, stored safely off-site in a safe-deposit box. Digital photos can also be backed up on a photo website such as Snapfish or Shutterfly. Or, even better, invest in an online backup service like Carbonite to protect precious digital photos, or store copies on an online "cloud" service like Dropbox.

5. CONTAIN & LABEL

The time investment to sort photos can be huge, so it makes sense to ensure they're preserved for generations to come by using archival-quality storage materials. Some types of storage include photo storage boxes, accordion file boxes, 3-ring binders filled with photo sheets, and heavy-duty plastic (poly) envelopes. Local office supply or scrapbooking stores will have a variety to choose from. Whatever chosen, look for products that are acid-free, archival, lignin-free, and PVC-free.

While sorting photos, recognize that oils from fingers can degrade photos and negatives so use care or wear gloves when working with cherished, old family photos. Paper clips, rubber bands, glue, and tape shouldn't be used unless they are specifically labeled as photo-safe.

Remember, not everyone wants their photos stored in binders or scrapbooks. For some, simply getting them roughly categorized by date or event and into easy photo storage boxes is good enough. Labeled, tabbed dividers in boxes can create order while minimizing time spent on the project.

It may be helpful to label some or all of the photos on the back with the date, location, and/or names of people in the photos. Be sure to use an acid-free, photo-safe pencil or pen.

6. CLEAN UP & MAINTAIN

Sort photos that you put in the share box by recipient, and place them in envelopes with the recipients' names on them. If mailing them, address the envelopes now, or place them in the car if they are to be hand delivered. Take out the trash.

Create a plan to maintain the system. As new photos enter the home, sort and store them according to the new system. As new photos are developed, label photo envelopes with the date, location, and names of people in the photos so photo maintenance is a snap.

clutter &
maintenance
tips

Now that you've learned
a pro's tips to organize
any space in the home,
don't forget that
maintenance will be key.
Here's how to keep it neat
and figure out if something is clutter,
followed by some frequently
asked questions about the
organizing process.

how to keep it neat

You've sorted, edited, containerized, labeled, and found the perfect place for everything. Now comes the most important part: teaching maintenance habits. If this step is skipped, the space will quickly go back to being disorganized.

How should homeowners keep a space neat and organized? Perhaps they could take ten minutes each evening to return things to their proper homes. Maybe the "in/out" rule would be good to keep the piles of clutter from returning. If other people live in the household, they should learn the new set-up and be told how to maintain it as well. Does everyone clearly understand the new organization system? Perhaps you could create an index card that lists daily, weekly, and yearly maintenance and tune-up information. Discuss a follow-up schedule so you can check back after a week, a month, and several months down the road to see if anything needs tweaking.

Most importantly, professional organizers should watch for teachable moments during organizing sessions. In most cases, clients want to learn organizing techniques so they can stay organized for life. So as you're working together, tell them what you're doing at each step. Have them work alongside you, so you can see if they're understanding. Don't panic at the thought of being a teacher. You don't have to teach them everything you know. Just share the basics so they can process their stuff easily from here on out.

Some of the simple organizing principles are listed in the sidebar.

tips

keep similar items together

assign a home for every object

put away what you take out

use containers to group similar objects

label things so there's no confusion about where to put items

abide by the "in/out" rule: when you buy something new, discard something old

daily, weekly, monthly, and annual maintenance is key

if you're not a pro

Print out the list of tips in the sidebar, and tape it to the fridge. Make sure everyone in the household understands that these basic organizing rules will keep your newly tidied spaces in tip-top shape.

home maintenance timeline

Maintenance — the last step in the six-step organizing process — is imperative to keep a space organized, relevant, and comfortable. A handy home maintenance timeline is provided here and reminds homeowners to review, tweak, and maintain their home's spaces on a regular basis, ensuring organizing success. For a printable PDF of this timeline, simply visit www.timetoorganize.com/printables.

TIME AND SCHEDULES — WEEKLY
Each family should hold a short meeting each Sunday evening to review the upcoming week's activities.

LAUNDRY ROOM — ONCE A MONTH
The laundry room should receive a quick-tidy once a month, and laundry should never be allowed to pile up.

ENTRYWAY — QUARTERLY
Plan to give the entryway a tweak at the beginning of each season to keep it neat and filled with weather-appropriate outerwear. In addition, there should be a daily review and distribution of the contents of the "launching pad" basket, and the area should be kept tidy by hanging up coats and bags and putting away shoes and other outerwear.

BEDROOM — QUARTERLY
An organizing maintenance session should be scheduled quarterly, and the bedroom tidied daily.

OFFICE, PAPERWORK, COMMAND CENTER — QUARTERLY
The home office and command center should be organized on a quarterly basis. Paper must be managed daily. Mail should be sorted as it is received, and junk mail should be tossed immediately. Everything else should be sorted into the active or reference-only filing systems. Each time a file is opened to get something out, a 30-second review can be completed to see what can be tossed.

LINEN CLOSET — TWICE A YEAR
Each spring and fall, as warm-weather blankets and sheets are exchanged for cold-weather ones, this space should be reorganized.

BATHROOM — TWICE A YEAR

Twice a year, medications and make-up should be weeded, tossing anything expired or outdated. Ratty towels should be donated to a local animal shelter. Anything that has found its way into the bathroom that doesn't belong there should be redistributed.

CLOTHES — TWICE A YEAR

In early spring and late fall, the cold-weather and warm-weather clothing should be switched out. Anything that is dated or is simply never worn or loved can be placed into the donation box. Extra hangers can be donated or taken to the dry cleaners for reuse.

TOYS — TWICE A YEAR

Kids toys should be downsized every six months; donate any that are seldom-used but in good condition. A "new toy in, old toy out" system should be followed where some purging takes place before shopping. A 10-Minute Tidy-Up Time each evening will help keep toys in their place.

LIVING SPACE — TWICE A YEAR

A maintenance session should be scheduled semi-annually to maintain an organized living space. In addition, the living space should be neatened each evening during a 10-Minute Tidy-Up Time.

KITCHEN — TWICE A YEAR

Twice a year, expiration dates should be checked on canned and boxed foods and old items in the fridge and freezer should be quick-purged. In addition, the kitchen and all its accoutrements should be reviewed. Items to discard include anything broken and anything unused in the past 12 months. Make sure the storage systems still make sense for the entire household.

GARAGE, ATTIC, BASEMENT — TWICE A YEAR

These spaces should be reorganized on a semi-annual basis so that they don't become clutter catch-alls.

PHOTOS — TWICE A YEAR

As new photos are developed, photo envelopes should be labeled with the date, location, and names of people in the photos so that photo maintenance is a snap. Twice a year, purge photos on the quick-toss list, and put the keepers into albums or preferred storage method.

CRAFT AREA — ONCE A YEAR

Craft supplies should be sorted once a year, and anything that is no longer needed should be tossed or donated.

how to figure out if it's clutter

Decluttering can be a difficult process. Stuff has a sneaky way of defining and controlling us. We hold tightly to our possessions because they bear memories, cost a lot of money, or were supposed to fix a problem. If this stage of the organizing process is difficult, here are some things to consider.

IS IT CLUTTER?

Clutter is anything unnecessary and extraneous. It can be more than the physical clutter. Getting organized means clearing out the clutter in the mind, heart, and life. There are three questions you can ask to determine if something can be released.

1. *Is it beautiful?* A stunning piece of artwork enriches your life because it brings joy each time you see it. A gorgeous vase full of fresh flowers reduces stress and energizes your spirit.

2. *Is it useful?* You use your 12-cup coffee maker every day. You couldn't make it through the week without it. (Don't confuse this question with, "Will it be useful *someday*?")

3. *Is it loved?* The antique pocket watch from your grandfather is a precious reminder of him. Your favorite cashmere sweater makes you feel fabulous.

If you don't get a "yes" answer to at least one of these questions, it is clutter and should go!

WHY SO MANY CLUTTER KEEPERS?

Some people inherit the clutter-bug and fear of not having enough from their parents. Back in the days of the Great Depression and the World Wars, people justifiably saved just about everything because of scarcity and rationing. However, in this day and age, there is no reason to continue this thought pattern. Thinking something will come in handy "one day" is *not* reason enough to keep it.

Clutter can also help fill a void. It can help to hide loneliness, anger, fear, and other important emotions. It fills time and space and keeps us focused on things other than our

clutter assessment questions

Am I keeping something simply because it cost a lot of money?

Am I keeping it simply because it was a gift?

Am I keeping it because it fills a void in my life?

Am I being swayed by advertising to buy things I don't need?

Do I really have room for it?

Could someone else use it?

If I get rid of it, could I replace it if I had to?

What's the worst thing that could happen if I toss this?

problems. However, when we free the clutter, we'll free ourselves to deal with the real issues. Clutter can also be part of one's identity. Perhaps someone collects books because it makes them feel smarter, or they have a huge collection of something that defines them. Similarly, some people want to hide in their clutter. They use an abundance of "stuff" to shelter themselves from the outside world.

And some people keep clutter out of guilt. If something was given as a gift, it's okay to let go and pass it along to someone else who might enjoy it. This is not throwing away friends' kindness or love, but simply releasing unneeded items to make room for the things that matter most.

IS IT ADDICTION OR HOARDING?

Shopping is embedded in our culture. But sometimes it turns into an addiction. It becomes a compulsive disorder which brings a temporary high. This excessive, chronic, and impulsive behavior can destroy a person's finances and relationships. Help may come to overspenders in the form of Debtors Anonymous meetings, credit or debt counseling, and professional assistance from a therapist.

Then there are those who save. Some people save things, and some people save *everything*. When it gets to the point that a home is nearly uninhabitable, compulsive hoarding may be the culprit. People who suffer from this psychological condition see the value in every object, leading to the inability to get rid of things (even items of no value, such as old newspapers and food containers). Hoarding is more extreme than simply accumulating clutter. Hoarders may not be able to move around the home. Floor space may shrink to a single pathway. Hoarding restricts everyday activities like cooking, cleaning, or sleeping and severely reduces the quality of life. Hoarders may not even recognize the extremity of their surroundings. Or, if they do, they may refuse to let family and friends visit their homes for fear of being criticized. Help can be found by visiting the websites listed in the sidebar.

if you're not a pro

If you're having a hard time letting go of the clutter, enlist the help of a friend or professional organizer to offer an objective viewpoint. This person can offer support and ask the tough questions like, "Are you really going to use that?" and "When will you ever wear that again?"

frequently asked questions
FROM PRO ORGANIZERS...

WHEN IS A PROFESSIONAL ORGANIZER NEEDED?

Hiring a trained, experienced professional organizer can be helpful to anyone who desires some hands-on advice and guidance throughout the organizing process. Professional organizers offer objective viewpoints about the amount and types of clutter in a home and can create an action plan so the job moves forward at the desired pace. In addition, they offer mental and physical support during the clutter-reduction phase and offer suggestions for storage and room layout as the project moves forward. Generally speaking, if someone has tried to get organized on their own before, and it didn't work out, then it's time to call in a pro.

THE ENTIRE HOUSE IS A MESS. WHERE SHOULD I START?

When the entire home is overrun by clutter, one good place to start is the bedroom. Chances are, sleep is being disrupted because of the clutter, so organizing that space and creating a safe haven for rest and relaxation will jump-start the organizing process. If the bedroom doesn't need organizing, then start in the most-used room of the house, which is usually the kitchen. Or, start with a small project, such as the entryway or bathroom to get a feel for the six-step organizing process described in this book. A small, successful project can boost confidence for organizer and client alike and be a springboard for more complex organizing projects.

WHEN SHOULD I BUY THE CONTAINERS?

While finding the right baskets and bins for a space is important, it is not the first thing to focus on. Sorting, decluttering, and figuring out the most appropriate spot for a category of items come first. Containers are the icing on the cake. They make everything look pretty, and by labeling them, they become "homes" to particular categories of items. Let the container shopping/installing be the reward for finishing the first four steps of the organizing process!

HOW DO I GET PAST PERFECTIONISM, MINE OR THE CLIENT'S?

Michael J. Fox has a fabulous quote that says, "I am careful not to confuse excellence with perfection. Excellence, I can reach for; perfection is God's business." Keep that in mind throughout the organizing process. Trying to create the perfect system, find the perfect container, or get the perfect result will only stall you out. Strive for an *excellent* solution to any organizing dilemma and you'll both be thrilled with the outcome.

frequently asked questions
FROM NON-PROS...

WHAT ONE THING CAN I DO TO JUMP-START AN ORGANIZED DAY?

Make your bed every day, first thing, no matter what. Do it before you get dressed, before you head to the kitchen to make your coffee, and before you wake the kids. Pull the sheets straight, get the comforter or duvet just right, and fluff the pillows. There is something about doing this simple, two-minute chore that sets the tone for the day. Your bed will look beautiful and orderly. Everything that comes after that, all day long, will have to live up to this benchmark. You'll be more likely to put dirty dishes in the dishwasher, file paperwork, and hang up your clothing. Seriously. Give it a try and see what happens!

WHAT IF I CAN'T STAY FOCUSED ON THE ORGANIZING PROJECT?

If a project seems too big and overwhelming, start with something small. Clear out the old magazines from the rack. Tidy up the scraps of paper on the fridge or bulletin board. Clean out your purse or briefcase. Set a kitchen timer for 15 or 30 minutes, and dedicate that time to just that space. Don't jump from room to room during this time. If you find an item that belongs elsewhere, do not take it there until the timer goes off. (This is where the relocation box comes in handy. Just drop in anything that needs to make its way to another room, and distribute it later.) If you are still having issues with focus, consider asking a friend to help you stay on task, or contact a professional organizer to help you set and reach your organizing goals.

WHAT IF SOMETHING HOLDS AN EMOTIONAL ATTACHMENT?

It's okay to be emotionally attached to something. The problems begin when someone is emotionally attached to *everything*. Let your conscience be your guide. If a little voice is telling you to let it go, but your heart is tugging it back, you are probably hanging on to it for emotional reasons, not because you love it, need it, or use it. Ask, "Why am I keeping this?" If it was a gift, recognize that it is okay to release that gift to make space for things that are truly relevant in your life right now. The gift giver would not want you to feel obligation to keep something that you don't need or love. If something holds a pleasant memory, give it a place of honor and display it prominently. Boxes full of memories littering the attic are not being honored. Select a few that are especially important, and enjoy them. Let the rest go. If you feel you have too much stuff, set limits. For example, decide to keep only 20 figurines on display or one memory box full of your kids' baby clothing.

HOW CAN I TEACH MY KIDS TO GET ORGANIZED?

Parents with good organizing skills usually pass them along to their kids. This should be good incentive to make your household an organized one! Begin by making organizing a part of each day. It's important to teach kids that every item they own has a "home" where it needs to return to when they're done using it. (This is where labeling comes in handy.) Let kids know they need to be responsible for their own possessions. Establish simple routines like making their own beds and loading and unloading their backpacks each day. Have a ten-minute clean-up every night before bedtime. Also, teach decluttering skills. Help kids downsize toys, sporting equipment, books, collections, and clothing every six months. Talk to them about how it feels — and how important it is — to donate to local charities. Establish a "new toy in, old toy out" system where some purging takes place before shopping.

HOW MUCH DECLUTTERING IS ENOUGH?

The amount of space will dictate how much you need to downsize. Consider your organizing goals and the amount and type of storage space you have. For example, if you want to contain all your books to a 3 x 6-foot bookshelf, figure out how many will realistically fit there, allowing at least six inches of free space on each shelf for artwork or something pretty. Any books that don't fit that space need to go. Always remember that any type of storage space or container needs a little "breathing room" so it is easy to remove and add items to it. Drawers should only be about two-thirds full. Clothing on a closet rod needs a little wiggle room so it doesn't get wrinkles. Stacks within a cupboard need to be kept manageable so it's easy to access an item on the bottom of the stack. Just remember, you can find new and better ways to store your things thanks to a variety of organizing tools, but you have to be realistic about how much stuff can fit the space.

I'VE TRIED TO GET ORGANIZED AND IT NEVER STICKS. WHY?

It could be that you haven't set goals for the space at the beginning of the project. It's hard to figure out where to go when you don't have a plan. Or perhaps you haven't committed to the last step, which involves regular maintenance. Try organizing one space using the six-step process in this book and try to keep it clutterfree for one month. If you are still having issues, a professional organizer will assess the situation and help you figure out why you are not meeting your goals. Perhaps Chronic Disorganization is a factor, which means you've struggled with this issue most of your adult life, have tried to get organized in the past, and still can't quite seem to make it work. You'll need more hands-on help, at regular intervals, but you will get there!

appendix

This appendix shares
comprehensive lists
of organizing tools and
where to buy them, plus
disposal options.

a dozen all-purpose organizing tools

There are literally thousands of organizing tools and products available in stores and online. The selection can actually be quite overwhelming! The following pages show some of the basics that will get you through many organizing jobs. Of course, discovering specialized tools for different areas of the home is half the fun, so spend time exploring organizing stores and product websites so you know what's available and current.

CLEAR, PLASTIC BOXES WITH LIDS

Stock up on these clear, lidded boxes. Brands such as Rubbermaid® or Sterilite® offer 6-quart and 16-quart sizes that are readily available for just a few dollars each. The small, shoebox size is nice not only for shoes, but also for accessories like belts, scarves, rolled ties, and small purses. (If you use a lot of them, check out The Container Store's discounted 20-pack of shoe boxes.) The 18 to 30 gallon tote sizes allow waterproof storage in the garage, attic, and basement. These boxes make storage on shelves neat as a pin and easily accessible. The functionality of clear plastic allows easy viewing of the contents without needing to open the lid, making retrieval a snap.

OPEN-TOP STORAGE BINS

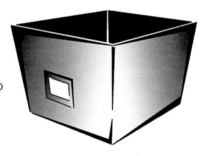

Open-top bins come in canvas, plastic, mesh, wood, rattan, and other materials to suit any decor and are available at a variety of price points. They are even available at many dollar stores. These are great for small pantry items, bathroom cleaning supplies, art supplies, toys, DVDs and CDs, and just about anything that needs to be corralled. The open top allows for grab and go convenience and makes clean-up time easy. Many come with a holder to insert a paper label. If not, it's easy enough to hang a tag to clearly designate the contents.

BASKETS WITH HANDLES

Handles make a storage container portable. Wicker laundry baskets, in particular, are an affordable, attractive storage option that can be used throughout the home. Watch for them on sale at your local discount or craft stores for less than $10. Put one at the bottom of the stairs. Then, throughout the day, drop in everything that needs to go upstairs, making evening clean-up quick and painless. Place one near the exit door for things that need to leave the house, such as clothing headed to the tailor or dry cleaner and library books and movies ready for return.

MAGAZINE FILE BOXES

Magazine file boxes can be found at a variety of price points to match any decor, from utilitarian cardboard or plastic to sophisticated bamboo or metal. These boxes can turn a pile of magazines, trade journals, or any periodicals into a unified collection. They can also corral school supplies like spiral notebooks and folders or be used in a Household Command Center. Many come with a metal label holder to make contents easily identifiable. Use them in the home office, the living room, or even the bedroom to disguise paper clutter.

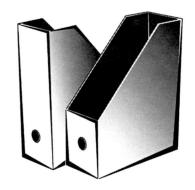

DRAWER DIVIDERS

This helpful product is an organizing super performer! Use them in the office to separate out rubber bands, paper clips, erasers, and other small office essentials. Stash them in the bathroom to hold cosmetics and first-aid items. Put them in kids' rooms to hold small toys or hair accessories. Sort out nails and screws in the workshop. Or, separate small craft supplies like beads and wires or sewing notions. Drawer organizers are available in a variety of price ranges, sizes, and materials (such as cardboard, clear acrylic, plastic, and bamboo). If you need maximum flexibility, look for one with adjustable or customizable compartments, so you can create the right-sized spaces for anything in a drawer.

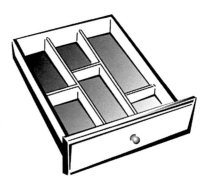

PHOTO STORAGE BOXES

Photo storage boxes are great for organizing more than photos! These inexpensive, versatile tools can be used to store crafts, office supplies, jewelry, small toys, bathroom doo-dads, recipe cards, and so much more. For less than $5 each, these boxes are an organizing best buy. They come in a variety of colors and patterns to match any decor. Label them clearly with a label maker or Sharpie pen.

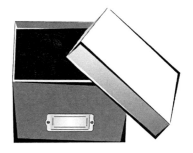

HOOKS OR HOOKRAILS

Hooks are helpful in a variety of spaces, including entryways, bedrooms, closets, laundry rooms, and garages. The Command™ Hooks (which come in white, black, and clear plastic plus attractive brushed nickel and oil-rubbed bronze finishes) are an inexpensive, easily removable option. For holding heavier items — like backpacks and jackets — a hookrail firmly mounted into a wall's studs is a sturdier option. Smaller hooks or hookrails can be used to make keys easily accessible on the way into and out of the home. Hookrails and hooks are a nice alternative for kids or grown-ups who don't like to hang clothing on hangers.

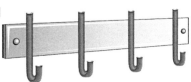

HANGING SHOE/OVER-THE-DOOR POCKET ORGANIZERS

Often hung on the back of closet doors for shoe storage, these organizers are wonderfully versatile. Hang one in a kids' room to store Barbie and her accessories or toy cars and trucks. Mount one on the wall near the baby's changing table to hold powder, diapers, and other necessities. Set up a gift wrapping station with ribbons, bows, tags, tissue, cards, and tape. Place one in the front hall closet to hold out-the-door necessities like umbrellas, sunglasses, work IDs, and lint rollers. Hang one in the pantry to corral snacks, cleaning supplies, or utensils. Choose clutter-hiding canvas or easy-to-see-through clear vinyl, depending upon your needs.

HANGING CANVAS SHELVES/SWEATER ORGANIZER

Available in a variety of colors, sweater organizers hang from a closet rod to use vertical space to the max. Use them in the bedroom closet to hold folded clothing like sweaters and T-shirts, or stash accessories like purses, belts, and hats. Get shoes off the floor by popping them into a narrower version of this organizer that holds ten pairs. These can also keep much-needed items at your fingertips. Hang one in the front hall closet to keep outerwear — such as hats, mittens, baseball caps, sunscreen, camera, dog leash, binoculars, and umbrellas — ready to grab on the way out the door.

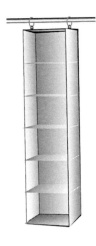

ROLLING/DRAWER CART

These drawers help utilize unused lower space beneath shorter garments hanging in the closet. They are great for underwear, socks, T-shirts, night clothes, and accessories in the bedroom or mittens, hats, and scarves in the entryway closet. Or try one to store art supplies, gift wrap, or scrapbooking papers. You can even create a mobile office or bill-paying station that can be wheeled from room to room. They are available with and without wheels in a variety of heights and widths.

CUBBIES

Cubbies (sometimes called cube organizers) offer a multitude of storage options. The most obvious use is storing shoes in a closet. But a small-sized cubby could be used as a mail sorter in the command center or home office. In the toy room or living room, each cubby square can be equipped with canvas storage bins that pull out for play time (labeled, of course, for easy retrieval and clean-up) or used as a bookshelf, each cube holding a different category of books. There are even cubbies that come topped with a padded bench for sitting, perfect for holding cold-weather gear in the entryway or mudroom.

TURNTABLE

Often used to hold jars of spices, the turntable (sometimes called a Lazy Susan) is helpful in a variety of other ways. Keep a single turntable in the fridge to hold condiments or cans of soda. Use a double turntable in a kitchen cupboard to make canned goods easily accessible. Stash a single, heavy-duty Lazy Susan under the kitchen sink or in lower cabinets to hold cleaning supplies. They can even be used to corral art supplies or to contain bathroom counter clutter.

organizing tools recommended in this book

- bins/boxes/baskets that are open-top
- bins/boxes/baskets with lids
- bookends
- bulk food storage containers
- bulletin boards
- cabinet risers/expanding shelves
- cabinet shelves
- cleaning caddies
- clipboards
- cubby organizers, large or small
- desktop step files, file sorters, or file boxes
- document/office storage boxes
- double hang closet rods
- drawer dividers
- drying racks
- hangers: wooden, velvet/no-slip, tube, pants, padded
- hanging overdoor shoe bags
- hanging sweater bags
- hooks, hookrails, over-the-door racks
- key racks
- laundry baskets and/or sorting hampers
- letter trays
- lid organizers

- magazine file boxes
- magazine racks
- multimedia boxes
- paper sorters
- pegboard
- photo boxes
- plastic stacking drawers
- rolling or storage carts/chests
- shelf dividers
- shelving/floating shelves
- shoe storage: floor racks, hanging shoe racks, shoe trees, shoe cubbies
- spice racks
- stacking bins
- stacking shelves
- trash cans
- turntables
- trays
- umbrella stands or urns
- underbed storage boxes
- undershelf baskets
- undersink pull-out baskets
- undersink, two-tier sliding organizers
- wall file/racks
- vacuum-sealed "space bags"

recommended organizing supplies

Having the right tools will make any organizing job easier. The following is a list of take-along supplies for the professional organizer.

BUSINESS TAKE-ALONG ESSENTIALS
- clipboard with fill-in assessment form
- breath mints, water, tissues, energy bar, band-aids, hand sanitizer, and cell phone
- receipt book or blank receipts
- extra business cards
- a camera (for before & after photos)

BASIC TAKE-ALONG SUPPLIES
- label maker plus extra cartridge tape and batteries
- pad of lined paper, pad of graph paper
- pens, pencils, felt-tip pens, Sharpies®, and highlighters
- office necessities like a stapler, tape, paper clips, scissors, labels, calculator, sticky notes, etc.
- box cutter, letter opener
- zip ties, cable ties, or cable clips
- tape measure and small tools (hammer, screw driver, level)
- assortment of nails and picture-hanging supplies
- Moving Men® furniture sliders
- cleaning rag or wipes
- gloves and dust mask (for very dirty or unsanitary circumstances)
- zip-top bags and garbage bags (heavy-duty, black)
- a few large cardboard or plastic boxes or baskets to assist with the sorting phase

OFFICE OR PAPER ORGANIZING BASIC SUPPLIES
- all of the above basic organizing supplies
- one box each of colored and manila file folders
- a box of hanging files
- a box of white labels for file folders

if you're not a pro

Even if you're organizing solo, make sure to have the basic supplies on hand to ensure smooth sailing. There is nothing worse than having to stop mid-project because you don't have a box cutter or extra label maker cartridges!

where to buy organizing tools & supplies

Whether you live in a large metropolitan area or in a small town, there is always some place to purchase basic organizing supplies. Homegoods stores like Target and Walmart are great starting points, and even local hardware stores and five and dimes will have some of the things you may need. But to really make the best use of space, you'll sometimes have to venture to an organizing product store (like The Container Store) or search out what you need via the internet. If you haven't been a fan of internet shopping in the past, now is the time to give it another try. The sites are generally easy to search, and many offer free shipping with a minimum purchase. Following is a listing of both brick and mortar stores and online stores that will provide just about any organizing tool you'll ever need.

GENERAL SUPPLIES

Ikea: www.ikea.com
Target: www.target.com
Walmart: www.walmart.com

ORGANIZING PRODUCTS

Amazon: www.amazon.com
Bed, Bath & Beyond:
  www.bedbathandbeyond.com
The Container Store:
  www.containerstore.com
Crate & Barrel: www.crateandbarrel.com
Current: www.currentcatalog.com
Lillian Vernon: www.lillianvernon.com
Linens-n-Things: www.lnt.com
Michaels: www.michaels.com
Organize.com: www.organize.com
Organize-It: www.organizeit.com
Organized A to Z: www.organizedatoz.com
Pottery Barn: www.potterybarn.com
Rubbermaid: www.rubbermaid.com
Stacks and Stacks:
  www.stacksandstacks.com
Solutions: www.solutions.com
Storables: www.storables.com

GENERAL OFFICE SUPPLIES

Avery: www.avery.com
Office Depot: www.officedepot.com
Office Max: www.officemax.com
Quill: www.quill.com
Staples: www.staples.com

BEAUTIFUL OFFICE SUPPLIES

Levenger: www.levenger.com
russell + hazel: www.russellandhazel.com
See Jane Work: www.seejanework.com

HOME IMPROVEMENT/CLOSETS

California Closets:
  www.californiaclosets.com
Easy Closets: www.easyclosets.com
Home Depot: www.homedepot.com
Lowe's: www.lowes.com

SCRAPBOOKING

Archivers: www.archiversonline.com
Creative Memories:
  www.creativememories.com
Michaels: www.michaels.com
Scrapbook.com: www.scrapbook.com

disposal options

There are many disposal options. It's a good idea to figure out disposal preferences before you start digging into an organizing job.

DONATE
Donating items in good condition to a local charity provides a tax-break incentive and helps others in need. Some organizations, such as Vietnam Veterans of America, offer pick-up service. Do an internet search to find the options in your area.

GIVE TO FAMILY/FRIENDS
Sharing meaningful treasures with loved ones is a way to make sure heirlooms and sentimental items go to a good home. But be aware that it's okay for people to decline the offers. Remember, we don't want to add clutter to others' lives!

GARAGE SALE
If there is a large amount of good-condition cast-offs (especially baby and kids' items, tools, or other highly desirable stuff), sometimes holding a garage/tag sale is a money-maker. But be aware of the amount of work that goes into the set-up, sale monitoring, and clean-up.

EBAY
Computer-savvy and hoping to make some money? Try listing furniture, antiques, and other higher-value items online at www.ebay.com. Or take treasures to an antiques dealer.

FREECYCLE/CRAIGSLIST
With more than 4,000 groups across the globe, the nonprofit Freecycle connects people who are giving and getting stuff for free in their own towns. Its mission is to reduce waste, save precious resources, and ease the burden on landfills. Visit www.freecycle.org for details. Craigslist (www.craigslist.org) is another no-cost listing service to try. It allows both giveaways and sale of items without any price bidding.

TRASH
Rent a dumpster if there will be a lot of unsalvageable junk. Or hire 1-800-GOT-JUNK®, North America's largest junk removal service. They load the truck, and then recycle and dispose of stuff as required. For smaller loads, consider the Bagster®, which can be purchased at many local home improvement stores, loaded with up to 3300 pounds of waste, and then picked up at your convenience for an additional charge. If you are doing the removal, remember to recycle when possible; learn the recycling guidelines in your area. And don't forget that household hazardous waste needs to be handled appropriately.

filing categories

Setting up a filing system is unique for each household. There is no one right way to do it. On the next two pages, you'll find one way to set up a system.

Generally, the fewer main filing categories, the better. (These are the ones that go on the hanging file folders inside a filing cabinet or file box.) You'll find these listed on this page. They are broken out into three broad categories of Financial, Family, and Home.

Then, within each hanging folder, you might have additional subcategories put into manilla or colored file folders. For example, the Credit Card hanging file might have three file folders within it if the family owns three different credit cards. You'll find those listed on the following page. Remember, there is no one-size-fits-all filing system. Use this as a starting point, and customize it to fit your family. If you'd like to print them out on cardstock, you can find this list available at www.timetoorganize.com/printables.

financial	family	home
AUTOMOBILES	EDUCATION	DECORATING
BANKING	EMPLOYMENT	HOME IMPROVEMENT
CREDIT CARDS	FAITH	HOME INSURANCE
INVESTMENTS	HOBBIES	MANUALS/ WARRANTIES
LEGAL/WILLS	INSURANCE: MEDICAL	MORTGAGE/RENT
REAL ESTATE	INSURANCE: DENTAL	PROJECTS
RETIREMENT	INSURANCE: LIFE	RECEIPTS
PAYCHECKS	INSURANCE: DISABILITY	UTILITY BILLS
TAXES	MEDICAL LABS/ REPORTS	

financial subcategories	family subcategories	home subcategories
car #1	school: child #1	phones
car #2	school: child #2	cable/internet
checking account	school: child #3	garbage
savings account	school: child #4	water/sewer
credit card #1	employment: mom	gas/electric
credit card #2	employment: dad	subscriptions
other credit cards	medical dad	
401 K	medical mom	
mutual funds	medical kid #1	
stocks/bonds	medical kid #2	
cds/money market	medical kid #3	
pension	medical kid #4	
social security		
current year's taxes		
donation receipts		

conclusion

Here are a few words
of inspiration to carry
you through your
organizing projects,
as well as how to learn more
about organizing or a
career as a professional organizer.

organization inspiration

Out of clutter, find simplicity.
— Albert Einstein

To know where you have enough is to be rich.
— Lao-Tzu

Life is really simple, but we insist on making it complicated.
— Confucius

Order is the shape upon which beauty depends.
— Pearl S. Buck

A place for everything, everything in its place.
— Benjamin Franklin

Happiness is a place between too little and too much.
— Finnish proverb

Simplicity is the ultimate sophistication.
— Leonardo da Vinci

Simplicity, carried to an extreme, becomes elegance.
— Jon Franklin

The more you have, the more you are occupied. The less you have, the more free you are.
— Mother Teresa

It is not enough if you are busy. The question is, "What are you busy about?"
— Henry David Thoreau

The more simple we are, the more complete we become.
— August Rodin

Simplicity is making the journey of this life with just baggage enough.
— Charles Dudley Warner

Have nothing in your houses that you do not know to be useful or believe to be beautiful.
— William Morris

how to learn more

Do you want to continue learning? Here are some opportunities to continue where this book leaves off...

BECOME MORE ORGANIZED

Would you like to receive helpful organizing tips via email? Visit www.timetoorganize.com to sign up for the free *Tips to Maximize Your Space and Time* newsletter. The website also includes a listing of donation and recycling resources, recommended reading, a "What's Your Organizing Personality" quiz, and helpful products (such as the *10-Minute Tidy-Up Tasks Organizing Cards* and *The Busy Mom's Guide to Getting Organized*) to move you on the path to an organized life. And don't forget to check out Sara's Pinterest page for hours of organizing inspiration, and then follow the conversations on Facebook and Twitter.

BECOME A PROFESSIONAL ORGANIZER

Contact Sara at Time to Organize if you'd like to learn more about organizing as a career. Visit www.timetoorganize.com/career to read details about phone and email coaching programs, ready-to-use *Essential Client Forms*, and the *Born to Organize* career guide. You can also sign up for the free, quarterly *Career Dreams* e-newsletter created just for career explorers.

GROW YOUR ORGANIZING BUSINESS

Time to Organize offers a variety of ready-to-use marketing tools for professional organizers, such as *Girls' Night Out Organizing Workshop Kits*, *Articles on Demand*, *Organize Today Client Newsletter*, *Stay-in-Touch Client Postcards*, *Facebook Posts on Demand*, and more! For information or to sign up for the free, monthly *Marketing Made Easy* e-newsletter, visit: www.timetoorganize.com/marketing.

about the author

"Anything is easy when you know how to do it." That's advice Sara Pedersen received from her grandfather many years ago. With the help of those encouraging words, she founded Time to Organize® LLC in 2000. After years of teaching Twin Cities residents to organize, simplify, and discover time to do the things they love, she now shares her knowledge with prospective and new professional organizers as a career coach. She is able to teach them how to do it, making it easy to launch new, successful careers as professional organizers.

Sara has a B.A. in journalism from the University of Minnesota. She has worked in print production, project management, and marketing communications roles, and she currently uses those skills by offering marketing services and products for professional organizers.

Sara is an active member of the National Association of Professional Organizers (NAPO) and the Minnesota chapter of NAPO. She has held the positions of Secretary, Newsletter Editor, Public Relations Director, and Electronic Communications Chair for NAPO-MN. She is also currently an Ambassador for NAPO at a national level and a member of the elite Golden Circle of NAPO for veteran professional organizers.

CONTACT SARA
phone: 651-717-1284
email: sara@timetoorganize.com
website: www.timetoorganize.com

CONNECT VIA SOCIAL MEDIA
facebook: www.facebook.com/timetoorganize
twitter: www.twitter.com/SaraPedersen
linkedin: www.linkedin.com/in/sarapedersen
pinterest: www.pinterest.com/saraped

notes